COMING TOGETHER OR PULLING APART?

THE EUROPEAN UNION'S STRUGGLE WITH IMMIGRATION AND ASYLUM

DEMETRIOS G. PAPADEMETRIOU

INTERNATIONAL MIGRATION POLICY PROGRAM
CARNEGIE ENDOWMENT FOR INTERNATIONAL PEACE

Coming Together or Pulling Apart?
The European Union's Struggle with Immigration and Asylum
(ISBN 0-87003-116-3/$8.95)
may be ordered from:
The Brookings Institution
Department 029
Washington, D.C. 20041-0029, USA
Tel. 1-800-275-1447 or 202-797-6258.
Fax 202-797-6004.

Cover and series design: Paddy McLaughlin Concepts & Design.

CONTENTS

LIST OF FIGURES

COMING TOGETHER OR PULLING APART?

THE EUROPEAN UNION'S STRUGGLE WITH IMMIGRATION AND ASYLUM

1. INTRODUCTION

After nearly two decades of neglect, immigration, refugee, and asylum issues have forced their way to center-stage on advanced industrial Europe's policy agenda. Among the many factors that have come together to propel these issues to prominence are the following:

(a) The angst that closely followed the euphoria associated with the Soviet bloc's collapse—particularly as Europeans worked themselves up to a virtual frenzy over the prospect of masses of former Soviet bloc citizens fleeing economic collapse and civil conflict, destabilizing Western Europe and undermining its prosperity;

(b) The conflict in the former Yugoslavia, which brought home to every European household not only "Europe's" impotence in resolving the conflict, but also its lack of immunity from the consequences—particularly the tide of refugees, which exposed Europe's vulnerability to large-scale migrant inflows;

(c) The unresolved social, cultural, and economic integration questions stemming from the foreign labor recruitment schemes of the mid-1950s to mid-1970s;

(d) The very real challenges of irregular[1] immigrants and (mostly fraudulent) asylum seekers coming from and through the East, as well as from the South; and,

(e) The pessimism associated with the faltering economic growth that followed the unusually long economic upswing of the late 1980s and early 1990s.

---

[1]This is a euphemistic term of art often used in European literature to denote illegal (unauthorized or undocumented) immigration flows.

1

There is also an even more fundamental reason for the intensity with which immigration, refugee, and asylum issues resonate in advanced industrial Europe. The issues impinge upon Europe's larger quest to redefine itself as an entity—the European Union (EU)—that amounts to much more than the sum of its parts. Several European governments are unwilling to surrender their sovereign prerogative to act unilaterally on such migration questions as: which non-Union nationals to admit and under what conditions; what rights to guarantee to such persons and how to integrate them; and how to prevent unwanted influxes (particularly influxes of asylum seekers). The failure to achieve consensus on how to manage migration has become one of the most serious obstacles to Europe's effort to build a deeper sense of "community."

The effort to achieve such a community grew out of Jean Monnet's post–World War II vision of an integrated Europe that would start to coalesce around the resolution of basically technical problems and then move toward ever closer association (Monnet 1978). The European Union,[2] that effort's current institutional expression, was created by the Treaty on European Union (TEU, or "Maastricht Treaty") as the successor to the European Community (EC) and related institutions (see box **1-1**, p. 3, for a review of the evolutionary "titles" of the Community.) The Maastricht Treaty's central vision is a Europe without internal borders, where goods, services, capital, and *persons* are able to move freely across national frontiers. Yet four years after the Treaty's signature and more than two years after its entry into force, failure to resolve the issues surrounding the ability of persons to move freely has become one of the largest items blocking the Treaty's full implementation. Indeed, implementation cannot be fully realized—administratively, much less politically—without first resolving such vexing immigration-related questions as the rights of non-EU nationals who are legally resident in an EU member state, citizenship and naturalization criteria, visa requirements, and external border controls.

These problems are not merely technical; they involve much larger socio-cultural and political issues. Their resolution will not be easy. Yet they must be resolved before European integration can

---

[2]As of this writing, the European Union has fifteen member states—Austria, Belgium, Denmark, Finland, France, Germany, Greece, Ireland, Italy, Luxembourg, the Netherlands, Portugal, Spain, Sweden, and the United Kingdom.

1-1. FROM ECSC TO EU— WHAT'S IN A NAME?

The European Coal and Steel Community Treaty was signed by France, West Germany, Italy and the "Benelux" countries (Belgium, the Netherlands and Luxembourg) in Paris in 1951. It is also referred to as the "Treaty of Paris." The six countries were referred to collectively as the *European Coal and Steel Community (ECSC)*.

In 1957, the same six countries signed the Treaty establishing the European Economic Community (also referred to as the "Treaty of Rome" or "EEC Treaty") in Rome; thereafter, the countries were collectively referred to as the *European Economic Community (EEC)*, although the EEC was additional to and did not replace the European Coal and Steel Community. Much of the discussion in this essay is concerned with developments within this Community, now much enlarged. A second treaty, signed in Rome in 1957, established the *European Atomic Energy Community (Euratom)*, again consisting of the same six countries.

In 1965, the so-called "Merger Treaty" fused the institutions of the three Communities—the EEC, ECSC, and Euratom—into a single governing group, headed by a single Commission (replacing the ECSC's High Authority and the Euratom and EEC Commissions) and a common Council of Ministers. The three Communities became collectively known as the *European Communities*.

Although many officials and analysts (inaccurately) continued to refer to the European Economic Community as the European Community, or EC, the official change in the designation of the European Communities to the European Community—intended to symbolize the movement beyond economic union to a more integrated political union—did not occur until the Treaty on European Union (TEU or "Maastricht Treaty") was signed in 1992. Under Title II, Article G, of the TEU, the official name of the EEC Treaty was amended to the "Treaty establishing the European Community" (or "EC Treaty"). The three original Communities (ECSC, EEC, and Euratom) together form the first pillar of the European Union, and are collectively referred to as the *European Community (EC)*. The *European Union* refers collectively to the Union's first, second, and third pillars—*the EC, Common Foreign and Security Policy (CFSP), and Cooperation in the Field of Justice and Home Affairs (JHA), respectively.*

Sources: European Communities 1987 and 1992.

become a reality. Failure to agree on a common visa regime or on uniform external-border management policies, for example, interferes with the Union's ability to implement its free internal-movement objectives. Similarly, and quite apart from its intrinsic merits, the fullest social integration of non-EU nationals is a practical necessity if several other Union objectives are to be attained. At a minimum, the long-term social cohesion of the Union clearly would be undermined by the presence of large immigrant communities—across the entire Union—whose members possess abridged, or even merely inconsistent, social and economic rights, not to mention unequal opportunities for full political membership.

What follows is an account of the labyrinthine and often tedious efforts of the European Community, and later the Union, to find a collective voice on immigration, refugee, and asylum policy issues over the past decade. This account not only documents a complex historical record, but analyzes Europe's continuing evolution toward a new developmental stage whose full dimensions are not yet clear. It tells the story of an ongoing, ambitious experiment by a group of states—an experiment taken up with varying degrees of enthusiasm—to devise nothing less than a new, collective identity for themselves.

In a narrower sense, this essay also provides an account of the effort—inspired in large part by the broad European vision and extraordinarily dynamic leadership of Jacques Delors, who served as the European Commission's President from January 1985 to January 1995—to develop a comprehensive Community approach to immigration and asylum. In keeping with that vision, the effort focused as much on integrating long-term residents of non-EU origin (and their descendants) into their receiving societies as on regulating admission and control of unwanted flows into Community/Union space. Most recently, it also focused on understanding and seeking to address the root causes of these flows. This dual-track approach—on the one hand working with member states to curb both authorized and unauthorized entry into EC/EU territory and, on the other, promoting the integration of non-EU foreign populations already legally resident—has characterized the Community's effort as well as that of most member states during and following Delors's tenure.

By the early 1990s, however, as fears of an onslaught of refugees and asylum seekers grew, fueling an already awakened anti-foreign sentiment, the restrictionist thrust came to dominate

4

Community discussions, while the integrationist thrust fell by the wayside. As a result, the effort to integrate the region's non-EU nationals into an internal frontier-free space has recently been relegated to the realm of eloquent but nearly empty rhetoric, with several EU member states growing steadily more wary of relinquishing national control not just over national borders but over sensitive social and cultural policies as well. Today, as the Union has become fixated on bolstering its external frontiers by controlling unauthorized migration flows and managing immigrant admissions ever more closely, the substance of the policy debate *at the level of the Union* has been reduced to a dialogue of the deaf about how far to go in agreeing to and implementing measures aimed at integrating immigrants fully within Europe's space.

This study looks beyond the better known and more intensively examined *external* events that have propelled or hindered European union. It focuses instead on the *internal* factors within Europe itself—especially within Community structures—that have dictated the pace of integration. This focus springs from the belief that what will define Europe's future *qua Europe* is the interplay between the Community's central institutions and its member states—an interplay marked by shifts in momentum, often conflicting agendas, and fundamental disputes about authority (or "competence," in Community parlance) over broad policy areas. The unresolved argument over competence—where it should reside *and how it should be exercised*—continues to color virtually all immigration-related questions. Considering that there is ample (though not uniform) recognition that unilateral state policies aimed at controlling unwanted migration are far less likely to succeed than multilateral ones—particularly in a framework in which production factors are intended to move freely, and decisions about most traditionally sovereign functions are on an inexorable path to being made collectively, notwithstanding recent setbacks—should competence over migration matters continue to rest with sovereign national governments? Or should it rest with intergovernmental bodies comprised of national-government representatives? Or with the central institutions of the Community? The evolution of the EC/EU's responses to immigration-related issues is a story of the tensions among these three approaches. The broader context in which this evolution is occurring could hardly be more difficult—as migration flows, real and feared, and their associated consequences become entangled with the extraordi-

5

nary complications of building a new, *European* identity. Together, these processes are not just reviving concerns about national "identity"; they are redefining all conventional notions of it. They are also creating for most of Europe's governments a legitimacy crisis that is as fundamental as any they have experienced in the post–World War II period. These processes have also become lightning rods for popular discontent.

This story is at times difficult to follow. This is due in no small part to the Community/Union's tendency to bury its deliberations in a fog of bureaucratic "terms of art." In the EC/EU's heavily nuanced jargon, for example, policy *harmonization* is a much higher standard than either *coordination*, which can imply something as vague as an emerging commonality of views on any given issue, or *cooperation*, which can imply the mere act of being constructive participants in a process. In most instances, Europe's progress on immigration and related matters at best amounts to cooperation.

2. EUROPEAN INTEGRATION'S FIRST THREE DECADES

The movement toward European integration began forty-five years ago, when six Western European states—France, West Germany, Italy, and the three Benelux countries (Belgium, the Netherlands, and Luxembourg)—organized themselves into the European Coal and Steel Community (ECSC). Although economic in character, the motivation for regional integration was essentially political, stemming from the experience of two world wars and the history of Franco–German conflict. An integrated, economically interdependent Europe, it was believed, would help to dampen Franco-German rivalry, prevent future aggression by a re-armed Germany, and unite Europe in the face of the then-deepening Cold War.[3]

Having achieved measurable gains through the ECSC, the six countries pursued further integration by signing two additional treaties in Rome in 1957—the "Treaty of Rome" establishing the European Economic Community (EEC) and a treaty creating the European Atomic Energy Commission (Euratom).[4] The EEC involved the merging of additional economic sectors into a common market that would gradually ensure the free movement of

---

[3] Western European countries and the United States agreed that the best way to prevent future German aggression was to anchor the country to Western European and trans-Atlantic institutions. The ECSC grew out of a proposal by French Foreign Minister Robert Schuman to place the French and German coal and steel industries—the building blocks of each country's war-making capability—under a common authority. Schuman also envisaged eventual European political unification through the "spillover" effects of concrete economic cooperation.

[4] Euratom was intended to control the production of nuclear technology.

2-1. THE INSTITUTIONS AND MECHANISMS OF THE EUROPEAN COMMUNITY/UNION

The *European Commission*, based in Brussels, is a supranational body that currently consists of 20 Commissioners (designated by their respective governments) whose professional allegiances are theoretically independent of their national governments as they act in the Community's interest during their term(s) in office. (Beginning in January 1995, Commission appointments were extended from four to five years to coincide with the terms of the European Parliament. Commissioners may be reappointed). The Commission President is chosen by the Council (see below) for a two-year renewable term, and is responsible for setting the agenda of the Commission. He heads an executive-level body that makes proposals for directives and regulations (which, when approved by the Council, constitute Community law), prepares programs of action, and oversees the implementation of both Council decisions and treaty provisions. The Commission is the only Community body that can initiate legislation on EC matters, and is considered the "engine" behind the unification effort.

The functions and powers of the Commission have grown dramatically over time, particularly under the forceful leadership of Jacques Delors. This development, however, has taken place much to the chagrin of some member states who see it as usurping powers "properly" belonging to member states. In fact, the Commission now plays the role of an executive branch of government, although it does so in a setting in which the legislative branch is essentially powerless, the judicial branch has a predictable tendency toward empowering the European institutions further, and the "true" executive—the Council of Ministers—often stands in an uneasy relationship to (and in a considerable day-to-day power advantage toward) the Commission.

The *Council of Ministers* (also known as the Council of the European Communities/Union) whose Secretariat is located in Brussels, is the decision-making body of the Community. Intergovernmental in nature, the Council brings together the appropriate ministers from each of the member states (depending on the matter under discussion) and decides on proposals put forth by the Commission. Following the Council meeting in Maastricht, one representative of the European Commission also sits on the Council of Ministers, although this individual possesses no voting authority and is only expected to present the Commission's position on matters before the Council.) Member governments hold the presidency of the Council of Ministers for six-month rotations. (Thus, terms are referred to as the French Presidency, the German Presidency, etc. See box **2-2**, p. 11, for a list of recent presidencies.) As officials of their respective governments, the Council ministers represent their countries' interests within the Community; this makes the Council appear as an obstacle to integration when it fails to adopt unity measures. At times, ministers in the Council pursue policies at the European level that they are unable to attain at the national level.

The Council of Ministers takes many decisions through qualified majority voting, although unanimity is the norm in more sensitive issue areas. With the entry into force of both the Single European Act and the Treaty on European Union, majority voting was extended to include, *inter alia*, areas pertaining to the common market, regional policy, worker protection, and education. The Council of Ministers is the only body that is able to approve legislation.

The Council of Ministers is assisted in discharging its day-to-day responsibilities by the **Committee of Permanent Representatives, or COREPER.** The COREPER is composed of member-state officials holding ambassadorial rank and a large staff of civil servants from each member state. In addition to preparing the Council meetings, the COREPER also ensures that Council decisions are implemented by Community officials. The COREPER's authority stems from Article 151 of the Rome Treaty, as modified by Article 7 of the Merger Treaty and Article 4 of the Treaty on European Union. Article 4 reads: "A committee consisting of the Permanent Representatives of the Member States shall be responsible for preparing the work of the Council and for carrying out the tasks assigned to it by the Council."

The **European Council** is not provided for in the original Community treaties, but has met informally since the mid-1970s. It was formally recognized in the 1987 Single European Act. It is composed of the heads of state and government of each of the member states, and the Commission President. The Council meets at least twice a year, to coincide with the end of each member state's six-month presidency of the Council of Ministers. Although the Council of Ministers is responsible for most Community decision-making, the European Council plays a significant role in advancing new initiatives.

The **European Parliament** (EP), whose secretariat is located in Luxembourg, plays a largely advisory role on draft legislation prepared by the Commission. Its principal function is that of a "watchdog" to ensure that

2-1. continued

the Commission does not favor any one member state over the Community's interests. Europeans were given the right to elect their representatives to the EP directly, for five-year terms, in 1979. The Parliament's membership increased from 518 to 567 in 1994, reflecting the enlargement of the Federal Republic of Germany after unification; and to 626 in 1995, to reflect the entry of the Union's newest members. Members of the European Parliament are organized along party affiliation rather than national membership, and vote by party bloc. Like the Commission, the EP has been a strong proponent of European integration, and EP votes rarely reflect national loyalties. Indeed, European parliamentary elections are frequently used as opportunities to express dissatisfaction with incumbent governments and/or political parties throughout Europe.

Since 1993, the EP's powers have been enhanced, primarily in the budgetary process and "consent" functions. However, its modest gains in "reviewing" Commission initiatives and "approving" Commission nominees and the selection of the Commission President fall far short not only of virtually any definition of a democratic legislative body, but also of the wishes of a German-led majority of member states (who were unsuccessful at the 1992 Maastricht European Council in significantly expanding the Parliament's legislative and oversight powers). The EP can force the resignation of the Commission by a two-thirds vote, but possesses no parallel power over the Council of Ministers. Although there is widespread citizen support for enhancing the Parliament's powers, restrictions remain on this most democratic of the European institutions.

The *European Court of Justice (ECJ),* located in Luxembourg, interprets Community law and ensures that treaties are implemented fully and applied correctly by the member states and other institutions. The Court is composed of 15 judges (one from each member state) appointed for six-year terms. The Court's rulings are binding, and its judgments in the field of EC law supersede national laws. Like the Commission and the European Parliament, the ECJ has been an important player in the movement toward integration. Its judgments and interpretations have established a body of law applicable to EC institutions, member states, national courts, companies, and private citizens. Since 1988, to assist with its rapidly expanding caseload, a *Court of First Instance* (a lower court) has aided the ECJ in the resolution of disputes, although it is still possible to appeal such rulings to the full Court (see also box **2-4,** p.17).

Sources: European Commission Delegation to the United States, 1994 and 1996.

2-2. CHRONOLOGY OF EC/EU PRESIDENCIES AFTER THE SINGLE EUROPEAN ACT

TERM	PRESIDENCY	SUMMIT LOCATION
January–June 1985	Italy	Milan
July–December 1985	Luxembourg	Luxembourg
January–June 1986	The Netherlands	The Hague
July–December 1986	United Kingdom	London
January–June 1987	Belgium	Brussels
July–December 1987	Denmark	Copenhagen
January–June 1988	Germany	Hanover
July–December 1988	Greece	Rhodes
January–June 1989	Spain	Madrid
July–December 1989	France	Strasbourg
January–June 1990	Ireland	Dublin
July–December 1990	Italy	Rome
January–June 1991	Luxembourg	Luxembourg
July–December 1991	Netherlands	Maastricht
January–June 1992	Portugal	Lisbon
July–December 1992	United Kingdom	Edinburgh
January–June 1993	Denmark	Copenhagen
July–December 1993	Belgium	Brussels
January–June 1994	Greece	Corfu
July–December 1994	Germany	Essen
January–June 1995	France	Cannes
July–December 1995	Spain	Madrid

goods, services, persons, and capital.[5] In 1965, EC member states signed the Merger Treaty, which established the common institutions of the European Communities (see box 2-1, p. 8–10). Since then, there have been two major revisions to the Treaty of Rome: the Single European Act of 1986, which sought to accelerate the creation of a single market; and the "Maastricht Treaty," or TEU, which established the European Union in late 1993 (after overcoming unexpected ratification difficulties). Negotiations over a third major revision of the Rome Treaty are planned to begin in the spring of 1996 and are expected to last until mid-1997.

THE CHALLENGE OF IMMIGRATION

For all of the Community's undoubted accomplishments, Europe's advanced industrial democracies[6] have yet to confront, in either a comprehensive or a particularly thoughtful way, the key issue of immigration. This is all the more remarkable since Europe has had four decades of extensive involvement with immigration—partly through systematic foreign-labor recruitment from the mid-1950s to the mid-1970s, and partly as a consequence of very complicated post-colonial relations. (Figure 2-3, p. 14–15, shows the number and proportion of the foreign-born in selected European countries.) In fact, few other phenomena have played as important a role as immigration in promoting the region's economic prosperity—or been blamed more uniformly for its economic, socio-cultural, and political ills during periods of economic uncertainty and social and political self-doubt and pessimism.

Western Europe did not in fact begin to confront the issue of immigration from outside the EC *systematically* until the second half of the 1980s. Some would place this date as early as 1974, when the Commission circulated a set of proposals about migrant workers and their families. However, little else occurred in the decade that followed. It was not until the Soviet bloc's collapse exposed the region's vulnerability to potentially uncontrollable immigration flows from Eastern Europe and the former Soviet

---

[5] The Rome Treaty's goal of a customs union, involving the elimination of all customs tariffs and quotas between member states, was completed in mid-1968, a year and a half ahead of schedule.

[6] Here, I include all of Europe north and west of the former Soviet bloc, regardless of the specific way in which each sub-region has organized itself (i.e., the Nordic Council, the EC/EU, or the European Free Trade Association).

Union that member states began to really consider the value of harmonizing their immigration policies and the possibility of bringing these policies into the Community's institutional framework. Since then, and particularly in the last five years, there has been extraordinary activism on the issue—most evident in the proliferation of European and international fora and in the literally hundreds of on- and off-the-record meetings on the subject each year. Even so, the less charitable observer would argue that concrete results have been meager and, in some instances, troubling.

This record begs the following question: How could advanced industrial Europe have remained so unprepared to address the consequences of immigration after more than a generation of experience with very substantial immigrant flows? A large part of the answer lies with the fact that, despite overwhelming evidence to the contrary, many governments clung to the official line that they were engaged in only temporary foreign labor recruitment, not permanent immigration. Some countries, most notably Germany, have lately embraced this line with renewed vigor. However politically convenient these statements may be, or how convincing they may sound to some in these countries' electorates, *they are not supported by either history or contemporary realities.*[7]

All of Europe's advanced industrial democracies crossed the threshold from *employers of temporary foreign workers* to *receivers of permanent immigrants* some time during the past two decades. The fact that most of these countries did so without a deliberate official act—i.e., without the symbolism of a formal change in the status of these not-so-new newcomers and/or without explaining to their publics that such a transition had indeed taken place—does not diminish the actuality or the practical irreversibility of the transition. By declining to acknowledge this "new" reality and not devising policies to address it, Europe's leaders essentially ceded the immigration issue to demagogues of the right and sowed the seeds for a troubling resurgence of Europe's anti-immigrant voices.

---

[7] With the end of most foreign-labor recruitment programs in 1973-74, several countries initiated incentive programs to encourage foreign workers to return to their countries of origin. As such programs proved unsuccessful and foreigners continued to enter Western Europe through increasingly generous family reunification policies, *immigrant integration* became Western Europe's stated policy focus.

2-3. Foreign Population in Selected European Countries: Total number of foreign born, percentage of total population, and percentage of foreign population originating in EC[a]

(thousands and percentages)

	1975	1980	1985	1988	1989
Austria	244	283	304	344	387
% of total population		3.7	4.0	4.5	5.1
% of foreign from EC					
Belgium[b]	835	877	847	869	881
% of total population		8.9	8.6	8.8	8.9
% of foreign from EC			63.6	61.8	61.4
France[c]	3,402	3,714	n.a.	n.a.	n.a.
% of total population	6.6	6.8			
% of foreign from EC	54.3	47.7			
Germany[d]	4,090	4,453	4,379	4,489	4,846
% of total population	6.6	7.2	7.2	7.3	7.7
% of foreign from EC		33.7	31.0	28.4	27.4
Italy[e]	n.a.	299	423	645	490
% of total population		0.5	0.7	1.1	0.9
% of foreign from EC			30.8	25.4	22.8
Netherlands	351	521	553	592	642
% of total population	2.6	3.7	3.8	4.0	4.3
% of foreign from EC	44.2	32.9	29.2	26.5	25.4
Sweden[f]	410	422	389	421	456
% of total population	10	5.1	4.6	5.0	5.3
% of foreign from EC		18.0		15.0	14.5
Switzerland[g]	1,013	893	940	1,007	1,040
% of total population	16.1	14.1	14.5	15.2	15.6
% of foreign from EC		77.1	74.8	72.2	70.9
United Kingdom[h]	2,600	n.a.	1,731	1,821	1,812
% of total population			3.1	3.2	3.2
% of foreign from EC			46.0	48.4	44.3

[a] In this table the terms EC and, as of 1994, EU, apply to the 12 countries of the European Community (Belgium, Denmark, France, Germany, Greece, Ireland, Italy, Luxembourg, The Netherlands, Portugal, Spain, and the United Kingdom) irrespective of the countries' dates of entry into the Community. This designation does not include the three countries—Austria, Finland, and Sweden—whose membership in the Community became effective in 1995.

[b] In 1985, as a result of modifications in the nationality code, some persons who formerly would have been counted as foreigners were included as nationals. This led to a marked decrease in the foreign population.

[c] Population censuses taken in 1975, 1982, and 1990. In this table, data for 1980 reflect those gathered in the 1982 census.

[d] Data up to 1984 and for 1990 are as of September 30; data from 1985 to 1989 and in 1991 are as of December 31; data for 1994 are as of June 30. Data refer to West Germany up to 1990 and to both East and West Germany from 1991 on.

2-3. continued

1990	1991	1992	1993	1994	
456	533	623	690	714	**Austria**
5.9	6.8	7.9	8.6	8.9	% of total population
					% of foreign from EC
905	923	909	921	922	**Belgium**
9.1	9.2	9.0	9.1	9.1	% of total population
60.9	60.1		59.6	59.9	% of foreign from EC
3,597	n.a.	n.a.	n.a.	n.a.	**France**
6.3					% of total population
36.5					% of foreign from EC
5,343	5,882	6,496	6,878	6,991	**Germany**
8.4	7.3	8.0	8.5	8.6	% of total population
26.9	25.3	23.2	22.3	22.3	% of foreign from EC
781	897	924	987	899	**Italy**
1.4	1.5	1.6	1.7	1.6	% of total population
16.4	16.2	13.5	15.5	15.3	% of foreign from EC
692	733	757	780	774	**Netherlands**
4.6	4.8	5.0	5.1	5.0	% of total population
24.3	24.0	24.2	24.1	24.9	% of foreign from EC
484	494	499	508	537	**Sweden**
5.6	5.7	5.7	5.8	6.1	% of total population
14.1	13.6	13.3	13.0		% of foreign from EC
1,100	1,163	1,214	1,260	n.a.	**Switzerland**
16.3	17.1	17.6	18.1		% of total population
69.1	66.8	63.3	61.2		% of foreign from EC
1,723	1,750	1,985	2,001	1,946	**United Kingdom**
3.2	3.1	3.5	3.5	3.4	% of total population
42.4	42.3	39.6	36.0	40.7	% of foreign from EC

[e] Data are adjusted to take account of the regularizations that occurred in 1987, 1988, and 1990. The fall in numbers from 1989 results from a review of the foreigners' registers (removing duplicate registrations and accounting for returns).

[f] Some citizens with permits of short duration are not counted (mainly citizens of other Nordic countries).

[g] Numbers of foreigners with annual residence permits (including, up to December 31, 1982, holders of permits of durations less than 12 months) and holders of settlement permits (permanent permits). Seasonal and frontier workers are excluded.

[h] Numbers estimated from the annual Labor Force Survey.

n.a. = not available

Sources: SOPEMI, *Trends in International Migration* (Paris: Organisation for Economic Cooperation and Development), 1976, 1981, 1993, 1995); and Provisional Country Reports to SOPEMI, 1995.

Europe's current preoccupation with immigration must thus be assessed against the backdrop of inconsistent and ambiguous policies and administrative actions, ill-considered political rhetoric, official inertia, and a not insignificant amount of official political and economic opportunism (interspersed with intermittent periods of scapegoatism). At issue is whether the European Union can deliver on its promise of full European integration without reconciling the incongruity between the unfettered access to EU physical, economic, social, and, at the local level, political space enjoyed by Union nationals with the severely restricted rights and privileges of non-Union or "third-country" nationals (TCNs) who reside legally within that space.

EARLY STEPS: FREEDOM OF MOVEMENT FOR WHOM?

By the early 1970s, the free movement of Community nationals was virtually a non-issue. The Rome Treaty's basic guarantees of equal access, establishment, and employment for citizens of the then-six EC member states had been met, often ahead of schedule. These guarantees are enumerated in Articles 48-66 of the Rome Treaty[8] and are safeguarded firmly by European Court of Justice (ECJ) decisions. A 1968 Council Regulation on freedom of movement elaborated on these rights and outlined the specific rights of Community nationals to equal treatment in employment, wages, and other working conditions (Borchardt 1995:38). Derivative rights of family reunification were also gained as early as 1968 (Council Directive 68/360) and were reinforced by the decisions of an activist ECJ.[9]

In developing this body of Community law, the ECJ has consistently restricted the ability of individual member states to interfere with EC nationals' enjoyment of such rights (see box **2-4**, p. 17). In fact, in the most traditional terrain of state sovereign expression—issues directly affecting public health and security, as well as those involving the exercise of such governmental functions as

---

[8] The Rome Treaty addressed only the free movement of salaried workers (Articles 48-51) and providers of services (Articles 59-66).

[9] The definition of "family" is quite broad and includes both dependent children and dependent parents of EC nationals. The rights extended to family members of EC citizens who are also salaried workers have been routinely contingent on proof that such individuals have access to "suitable" housing. These rights also have been subject to customary restrictions on public policy, public security, and public health grounds.

2-4. JUDICIAL ACTIVISM IN THE EC/EU

The role of the European Court of Justice (ECJ) in consistently—even aggressively—defending and promoting the principles laid down in the Rome Treaty, is a frequently under-appreciated component of Europe's march toward "union." Yet it is a subject of much analytical and political debate whether the Court has expanded—or should expand—its areas of competence beyond those intended by member states.

The ECJ's judicial activism on integration matters is comparable to that of court involvement on immigration issues in the "traditional" immigration countries of the English-speaking world. The Court has almost invariably interpreted in the broadest possible manner such matters as family definition, family reunification (including associated labor market rights), and the rights to move, reside, offer a service and/or obtain work (as well as to gain access to social services and benefits) in any member state. Even on matters involving public sector employment, an extremely sensitive area, the Court has ruled that states cannot restrict the rights of nationals and their families unless there is a ". . . genuine and sufficiently serious threat affecting one of the fundamental interests of society." In cases of professional services, another politically and technically complex area, there has been progressive liberalization in favor of mutual recognition of diplomas and assessments of professional experience—a process that culminated in a 1992 directive setting up a full system in these regards.

Not all members states approve of the Court's judicial activism. The United Kingdom, in particular, holds fundamental reservations about the Court's reach and implications for national sovereignty.

Source: ECJ 1977.

police and public-sector employment—Community law and ECJ rulings have gradually and consistently narrowed states' rights.

In contrast, the rights to entry and free movement of third-country nationals have been far more restricted.[10] At least until recently, these matters were regarded primarily as the preserve of national governments.[11] As a consequence, the EC did not begin to devote attention to the issue of TCNs working and residing in the Community until 1974, and then only tentatively and in the broader context of *all* migrant workers. The initiative took the form of an **Action Programme** to address the problems of migrant workers and their families (see Commission 1991c:18). Many of the Commission's recommendations were approved in a 1976 Council Resolution, in which member states were also encouraged to adopt common migration policies toward non-member countries in "consultation" with the Commission (Callovi 1992:355-356).[12] Though devoid of specific proposals, the resolution marked the beginning of a recognition by the Council that a common response to a shared problem seemed both desirable and achievable.

At least two factors brought the TCN issue to the fore. After the 1973 oil embargo and the resulting recession, nearly all Western European governments ended their labor-recruitment programs, leading the EC Council of Ministers to ponder what to do with migrant workers legally resident in Community territory. Moreover, in 1974, the Community experienced its first enlargement when Denmark, the United Kingdom, and Ireland were admitted. This, and subsequent enlargements incorporating Greece (1981) and Spain and Portugal (1986), raised the issue of an expanded Community territory in which to consider the free movement of persons, and sparked interest in "hardening" the Community's external borders.

---

[10] It is important to note that the third-country nationals referred to in this essay are almost exclusively nationals from Third World countries. The rights of nationals from the countries in the European Free Trade Association (EFTA) were safeguarded throughout most of the period under analysis, as were many rights of nationals from other advanced industrial democracies, which tend to have an extensive network of bilateral agreements on these matters with most EU countries.

[11] The degree to which the issue is considered to be under the "exclusive" control of state sovereign action is under some dispute by those who point to the ECJ's activism on this issue (Niessen 1995).

[12] In March 1979, the Commission issued a communication to the Council seeking clarification of the terms of that consultation. As Callovi (1992:356) notes, the Council reiterated its preference for "appropriate" consultation but established no binding mechanism.

3. 1985–1991: HIGH HOPES AND COMMUNITY LEADERSHIP

ost of the discussion about immigration from third countries has revolved around two main axes: (1) the *integration* of immigrants already legally and "permanently" residing in EC territory, and (2) *controls and restrictions* on those seeking to enter the region.[13] As noted throughout this essay, issues of integration have long been an area in which the Community's *central institutions* (i.e., the Commission, the ECJ, and the Parliament) have shown significant interest and leadership,[14] whereas issues of control have been handled primarily on a unilateral and secondarily on an *intergovernmental* basis through the European Council. The tension between central institutions and intergovernmental bodies permeates Community discussion on immigration issues in Europe.

1985: PUTTING IMMIGRATION ON THE AGENDA

GUIDELINES ON MIGRATION

The first *concrete* attempt to develop a Community policy on migration took place in 1985, when the Commission issued, and

---

[13] In the minds of many national and EC policy makers, these two issues are inextricably linked. A key argument in favor of restricted immigration, for instance, is the assertion that continued admission of non-EC nationals into EC territory will impede the integration of immigrants already living in the area. Among the reasons commonly cited in this line of argument are limited public resources for supporting new influxes, decreased labor market capacity for absorbing new immigrant workers, and diminished public support for new admissions. For a discussion of that line of thinking in the United Kingdom, see Papademetriou and Hamilton (1996).

[14] In addition to the 1974 and 1976 Commission initiatives discussed earlier, Community interest in this area is evident from the following actions: the Commission Guidelines for a Community Policy on Migration (1985); a joint Council/Commission/Parliament Declaration against Racism and Xenophobia (1986); the Strasbourg Council's adoption of a Commu-

the Council adopted, its **Guidelines for a Community Policy on Migration.** In addition to reiterating the principles of free movement for Community nationals (particularly workers), goods, services, and capital, the Guidelines articulated the Community goal of attaining "equality of treatment in living and working conditions for *all* migrants, *whatever their origin.*" (Commission 1985a: 5,8; emphasis added).[15]

The Guidelines incorporated the conclusions of an earlier Commission assessment of member states' immigration policies, which had found that migrant communities in Europe were showing "every sign of establishing [themselves] permanently" (Ibid.:6). Significantly, the assessment had also identified a number of priority issues that needed attention before the larger Community goal of "European citizenship" could be realized. These included freedom of movement for TCNs and the need to regularize their status and remove all obstacles to equal treatment.

The Commission noted a number of common trends among member states. Among them were the consolidation of TCN communities despite a reduction in the numbers allowed permanent residence; growing concern about (and steps to control) illegal immigration and fraudulent asylum claims; increasing emphasis on social, cultural, and labor market integration for all foreign residents (including efforts to combat "xenophobia, intolerance, and racism" [Ibid.]); and continuing efforts to help migrants retain their ethnic and cultural identities with the aim of facilitating their voluntary return to their countries of origin.[16]

nity Charter of the Fundamental Social Rights of Workers (1989); a Commission report on the Social Integration of TCNs Residing on a Permanent and Lawful Basis in the Member States (1989); a Council Resolution on the Fight Against Racism and Xenophobia (1990); a Commission report on Policies on Immigration and the Social Integration of Migrants in the EC (1990); and a Commission White Paper on Social Policies (1994) which contained numerous proposals regarding the status of TCNs. Most integration matters regarding *Community nationals* fall explicitly within the Union's "competence" under the Treaty of European Union.

[15] It is important to note that the Commission did not have authority to act further on the issue. In fact, until the Single European Act was drafted in December 1985, no compelling common interest in harmonizing migration policies was recognized.

[16] This emphasis on "cultural maintenance" is complex and not necessarily the thoughtful and progressive policy it may appear to be. It is, in fact, the policy expression of Europe's fundamental ambivalence about immigrants, which allows some national leaders

These findings persuaded the Commission of the importance of focusing on the working and living conditions of third-country nationals. On July 8, 1985, on the basis of Article 118 of the Rome Treaty,[17] the Commission announced a Decision aimed at "achieving progress towards a harmonization of national legislation on foreigners" (Commission 1985b:19). The Decision introduced a procedure requiring member states to give the Commission and other member states advance notice of draft measures they intended to take toward third-country workers and their families "in the areas of entry, residence, and employment, including illegal entry" (Ibid.:20). Member states were also to provide related draft cooperation agreements they intended to (re)negotiate with third countries.

This initiative generated protests from several member states that were unwilling to grant even *consultative* license to the Commission with respect to TCNs. Germany, France, the Netherlands, Denmark, and the United Kingdom appealed the Commission decision before the European Court of Justice, arguing that migration policy toward non-member states exceeded the scope of the Commission's powers as envisaged by Article 118. They charged that the Commission lacked "competence" either to extend the consultation procedure to matters pertaining to the cultural integration of TCNs and their families or to require that national draft measures and agreements with regard to TCNs conform to Community policies and actions (ECJ 1987).

In a July 9, 1987 ruling the ECJ voided part of the Commission Decision, but this did not completely block the Commission's first significant attempt to "institutionalize" immigration matters. In fact, the Decision was later revised and adopted, and a consultation procedure was established. This "success" thus signifies the

---

to perpetuate the myth that "foreign workers" and their children intend eventually to return to their home countries—despite overwhelming evidence that they are in Europe to stay. With some exceptions (notably France and the Netherlands), the result has been the *de facto* segregation of immigrant groups, which has effectively delayed, and in many instances inhibited, their effective integration into the host community.

[17] All EC social policies have their foundation in Article 118, which specifically charges the Commission with promoting cooperation between member states in matters relating to employment, labor law and working conditions, vocational training, social security, and other social policies.

first instance of explicit Commission competence on immigration matters (Niessen 1992:681).[18]

THE SINGLE EUROPEAN ACT

The principal catalyst for increased intergovernmental cooperation on immigration policies among EC member states was the February 1986 signing of the **Single European Act (SEA)**, which entered into force on July 1, 1987. The Act marked the first major reform of the EEC's "constitutional" framework since the 1957 Rome Treaty. It was the first step in Commission President Jacques Delors's efforts to restore momentum toward integration by systematically attacking the remaining obstacles to the creation of a single market free of internal frontiers. In Delors's thinking, the move to abolish frontiers between EC countries would in turn convince member states of the need to cooperate on admission and other border control measures, thus creating a context for subsequent efforts to bring immigration policy into the institutional framework of the EC. Although the Act did not include mention of common immigration policies, Article 8a of the SEA set policy goals that, realistically, could not (and cannot) be fully realized without EC-wide policies on immigration.

In developing the SEA—and in a gesture revealing the significance of freedom of movement in member states' plans to establish a frontier-free Community space—the Council had asked the Com-

---

[18] The Court of Justice required two amendments to the Decision prior to its adoption. All "cultural" references were to be omitted, and states would not be required to submit drafts of their laws *prior to their adoption*. (The Commission had sought to institute a system of prior review to avoid opening an "infringement procedure" after a law's adoption [Callovi 1995]). This weakened consultation procedure constituted the sole area of Community competence on immigration matters until the entry into force of the Treaty on European Union (TEU). Member states, however, have continually resisted the measure and, even after the TEU went into effect, argued that it no longer made sense to have two overlapping consultation mechanisms—one based on Article 118, and the other on the third pillar (see Article K.3, TEU, discussed later in this essay). Thus, while the Commission could in practice require member states to comply with Article 118, the latter has been used principally to deal with matters of integration (de Jong 1995). The Commission did not issue another Decision on TCNs until June 8, 1988. At that time, it proposed even greater Community responsibility for policies toward non-Community workers, anchoring its renewed effort, at least partly, on the implications of the presence of such workers for a Community-wide employment policy. The 1988 Decision again made the case for harmonizing bilateral agreements between member-states and third countries and for focusing more directly on protecting the interests of Community nationals living and working in non-EC countries (see Callovi 1992:357). Despite its expressed intent, the Decision has been poorly implemented, and most of its provisions have been subsumed under Title VI of the TEU.

mission to assess the matter of internal borders. The resulting Commission White Paper, presented to the Milan Council in June 1985, discussed the importance of easing physical, technical, and fiscal controls at the Community's internal borders. It listed almost 300 legislative proposals for eliminating barriers, including an end to intra-EC customs checks and frontier controls, and offered a timetable for achieving the objective of a single market by the end of 1992 (hence Delors's designation of the initiative as "Europe 1992," or the even more widely used "EC92"). The White Paper's many recommendations included coordinating member states' refugee, asylum, and visa policies, and reaching agreement on the status of TCNs (Callovi 1992:358). The Council approved the White Paper and set up an Intergovernmental Conference to examine revisions in the Rome Treaty needed to establish the single market.[19]

ARTICLE 8A OF THE SINGLE EUROPEAN ACT

Most of the White Paper's sweeping proposals found their way into the Single European Act (SEA), signed by the heads of state and government in Luxembourg in February 1986. Article 8a of the SEA states that "the Community shall adopt measures with the aim of progressively establishing the internal market over a period expiring on 31 December 1992." It defined "internal market" as "an area without internal frontiers in which the free movement of goods, *persons*, services and capital is ensured" (European Communities 1987:544; emphasis added).

Disputes over how to interpret Article 8a arose immediately. The British and Greek delegations, for instance, insisted that the measure referred exclusively to member-state nationals (AHIG 1991a:33), while the Commission interpreted it more broadly to include non-Community nationals as well. In addition, at a conference in Luxembourg on September 9, 1985, member states adopted a general declaration reaffirming their national rights to

---

[19] Intergovernmental Conferences (IGCs) might best be compared to small "constitutional conventions" at which the Union's "constitution"—the Treaty of Rome—can be substantially amended. IGCs typically consist of periodic (often monthly) meetings of the EC member states' Foreign Ministers. Other ministers may also meet (and often do) on technical issues under their jurisdictions. The Intergovernmental Conference that prepared the Single European Act met from June 1985 to February 1986 (see Hix 1995 for a detailed discussion), while the one leading to the Treaty of European Union and the Maastricht Council commenced in late 1990.

determine immigration policies for TCNs. "Nothing in these provisions," they maintained, "shall affect the right of Member States to take such measures as they consider necessary for the purpose of controlling immigration from third countries, and to combat terrorism, crime, the traffic in drugs and illicit trading. . . ." (European Communities 1987:588). By the time the Single European Act was signed, all references to freedom of movement for non-Community nationals had been deleted.

Nevertheless, as the years following adoption of the SEA demonstrated, the goal of eliminating internal frontiers required the development of common measures for external border controls and short-term admission to EC territory. Therefore, although the Act did not create a common *immigration* policy, the implications of its priority objectives—particularly in the security realm—generated sufficient cause for subsequent attempts to bring immigration matters into the ambit of Community competence.

THE SCHENGEN "LABORATORY"

Motivated by the discussions surrounding the White Paper and the Single European Act, five of the original EC member states (excluding Italy) announced their intention to accelerate their own frontier-elimination plan, to be completed two years ahead of the EC92 schedule. On June 14, 1985, these countries signed the **Schengen Agreement**, a plan to eliminate internal frontiers among the signatories by January 1, 1990 (see box **3-1**, p. 26). A Supplementary Convention, signed on June 19, 1990, effectively extended this deadline to 1993. Like the SEA, the Schengen Agreement envisaged the removal of intra-EC borders *in exchange for strengthening the region's external borders.*

Although it was negotiated independently of the EC and has its own secretariat, the Schengen Agreement has come to be viewed by many as a laboratory for Community-wide efforts to eliminate internal border controls. The Commission has participated as an observer since the Agreement's inception and many subsequent conventions negotiated among EC member states—e.g., the External Frontiers, Dublin, and the European Information System conventions—have been modeled partly after Schengen.[20] It

---

[20] Once any of these conventions enter into force, the pertinent Schengen measures will cease to be valid (Callovi 1995).

24

soon became evident, however, that Schengen also served as a microcosm of the difficulties EC member states have encountered in their efforts to establish a frontier-free Community.

THE AD HOC IMMIGRATION GROUP

After the intensive activism of 1985, and with the goal now set firmly on complete freedom of movement of persons within EC territory, member states began to consider the possibility of coordinating their immigration and asylum policies in the context of establishing complementary border-control measures. At their first meeting in London in 1986, the Ministers Responsible for Immigration[21] created the **Ad Hoc Immigration Group of Senior Officials** (hereafter, Ad Hoc Immigration Group, or AHIG) as the organizational vehicle for pursuing cooperation on immigration policies (see box **3-2**, p. 28).

During the next two years, the AHIG attempted to devise measures and principles on visa policy,[22] external borders,[23] and common rules to determine the member state responsible for examining an asylum application.[24] Emphasizing the connections between border controls and immigration, the AHIG insisted that each member state consider measures necessary to compensate for potential security risks to the other members should its own external border policies fail. Thus if member states stopped relying

---

[21] Although the Interior and Justice Ministers of the EC member states had been meeting in various capacities prior to 1986, that year's London meeting marked their first as the "Ministers Responsible for Immigration." At the national level, none of the member states (Italy has been the only exception for a brief period in 1991-1992) have either an immigration minister (as do Australia and Canada) or a commissioner (as does the United States). In larger member states (the United Kingdom, Germany, Italy, Spain, and France), immigration issues are dealt with principally by the ministries of Interior/Home Affairs (with Labor and Social Affairs ministries a close second); in nearly all of the other member states, Justice ministries deal with immigration matters (Vos 1995). It is not always clear who has policy "primacy" on immigration matters—although interior/public order ministries (entities similar to the U.S. Department of Justice) seem to be gaining the upper hand as the issue is increasingly seen in the context of law enforcement.

[22] This included the drafting of a preliminary common list of countries whose nationals would require visas to enter and move within EC territory. At their 1987 meeting in Copenhagen, the Ministers Responsible for Immigration adopted such a list, which included fifty such countries (later expanded to include eleven additional countries at their Munich meeting in June 1988) (AHIG 1991a:11-12).

[23] This included controls at seaports and airports, and the development of a list of non-admissible TCNs.

[24] The latter culminated in the signing of the Dublin Convention in June 1990.

3-1. THE SCHENGEN AGREEMENT

The first "Agreement Concerning the Gradual Abolition of Controls . . . at Common Borders" was concluded at Schengen, Luxembourg, on June 14, 1985. The Agreement was intended to remove the internal frontiers among its signatories (Germany, France, and the Benelux countries) by January 1, 1990, two years prior to the anticipated removal of such frontiers among all EC member states.

The Schengen Agreement stemmed from the inability of EC member states to reach a Community-wide agreement on the removal of internal frontiers, in large part because of resistance (particularly by the United Kingdom) to relinquishing control over national borders. An important catalyst for the Agreement was a protest in the spring of 1984, in which truck drivers, fed up with long lines at the Community's internal frontiers, virtually halted movement across borders. The protest led the French and German governments to sign the Sarrebruck Accord in July 1984, ending the control of persons at Franco-German borders. These governments subsequently invited the governments of the Benelux countries—which had had such an arrangement in place since 1960—to join them in establishing the Schengen Group.

Because the parties to Schengen considered the Agreement to be a statement of intent, they did not submit it to their respective parliaments for ratification (with the exception of the Netherlands, whose parliament has ratified the accord). After they missed their deadline for the elimination of internal frontiers, the five original signatories and Italy signed a Supplementary Convention on June 19, 1990, and submitted it to member parliaments for ratification.

The Supplementary Convention provided for: dismantling internal border controls on the movement of goods and persons (irrespective of nationality) between contracting parties; establishment of common external borders; adoption of a common visa policy for short- and long-term stays by nationals of third countries; stronger internal controls (including procedures for the issuance of residence permits, a reporting mechanism for inadmissible aliens, and mutual cooperation and enforcement in criminal matters); and the creation of a common *Schengen Information System* (SIS) by January 1993.

The European Commission participates as an observer at the Schengen ministerial meetings and has been fully engaged in the Agreement's implementation. Portugal, Spain, and Greece have since signed the Agreement, and Austria, an "observer" since July 1994, signed in 1995. The United Kingdom, Ireland, and Denmark do not participate. Although Italy and Greece signed the Agreement, they have not yet satisfied the necessary preconditions for implementation and are thus excluded from the arrangement until they adapt their information systems to the SIS. The much-delayed SIS links the member states' information systems to a central system located in Strasbourg and allows for information exchanges on entrants into any Schengen member state.

Ratification by Schengen's signatories was held up by numerous concerns arising from the suppression of internal border controls, as well as by the insistence of some signatories that other members adopt equally stringent and thorough external border controls. Of particular concern have been the "porous" borders of some southern European countries, increased drug trafficking (and France's apprehension about the liberal drug policies of Spain and the Netherlands), and crime. Ratification was also impeded by a number of technical difficulties, such as the creation of an adequate policing system. An even greater obstacle, however, may have been growing concern about refugee and asylum flows into the region, which led some of the Agreement's initial supporters to continue to delay its implementation. Finally, privacy concerns associated with the SIS also held up ratification.

A trial period for implementation of the Schengen Agreement began in March 1995 (see pp. 95-97).

Sources: Cruz 1993, Callovi 1990, and Vos 1992.

3-2. THE AD HOC IMMIGRATION GROUP (AHIG)

The Ad Hoc Immigration Group (AHIG) was created in 1986 by the Ministers Responsible for Immigration to assist them in the discussion and development of common policies on immigration. Composed of senior officials below the ministerial level from member states' Justice and Interior ministries, or of other high-level officials responsible for immigration matters, the AHIG grew out of, but did not replace, the Trevi Group (described in box **3-3**, p. 32). The AHIG was staffed by the Secretariat of the Council of Ministers and aided by six smaller working groups on asylum, external frontiers, false documents, admissions, deportations, and information exchange. Although a representative of the Commission was included in the AHIG from the beginning, the Commission has possessed no right of initiative. The AHIG was replaced by the K.4 Committee's Steering Group I (Immigration/Asylum) after the Treaty on European Union entered into force in November 1993 (see box **5-1**, p. 76).

The Ad Hoc Group's mandate covered a broad set of issues. These included: (a) improving checks at external Community frontiers, and assessing the value of internal controls in combating terrorism, drug trafficking, crime, and illegal immigration); (b) evaluating the feasibility of harmonizing member state visa policies, and the effect such action might have on improving external controls; (c) examining methods for easing intra-Community travel without abetting terrorism, drug trafficking, illegal immigration, and other criminal activities; (d) developing measures (in consultation with both the Council of Europe and the U.N. High Commissioner for Refugees) to achieve a common policy toward the elimination of asylum abuse; and (e) addressing numerous operational issues, such as the exchange of information about spot-check systems and the prevention of passport abuse.

Source: AHIG 1991a.

on *national* controls for their internal security, effective compensatory mechanisms for tightening up controls at the Community's external borders would be required.

THE COMMISSION'S RETREAT

Notwithstanding the enhanced attention to immigration issues, coordination (much less harmonization) of member state actions at the Community level was a far more elusive goal. Although the Commission had previously taken the lead in pushing for the harmonization of national legislation toward third-country nationals, immigration matters for the most part remained outside the institutional framework of the EC.[25]

The abolition of internal frontiers, on the other hand, did fall under the Community's competence. Hence, to the extent that the Community considered immigration and asylum matters, it would have to do so within the context of the larger search for a political formula to achieve an internal frontier-free space. Thus, rather than taking on the full agenda of a comprehensive immigration policy that would address the rights of TCNs, the Commission opted for a narrower program aimed at the presumably more attainable objectives of harmonizing visa, asylum, and border policies. In this way, the Commission was able to sidestep fundamental questions of legal doctrine in favor of more practical matters.

Accordingly, in a December 7, 1988 Communication, the Commission proposed that Community legislation in the immigration area "be applied only to those cases where the legal security and uniformity provided by Community law constitute[d] the best instrument to achieve the desired goal" (cited in Callovi 1992:360). By thus acknowledging that intergovernmental cooperation would likely be the most practical vehicle for attaining EC92 goals, and by assigning to itself the limited role of informal, if active, participant in these deliberations,[26] the Commission set the stage for an undistracted and substantive discussion of the SEA's freedom of movement objectives. The December 1988 Communi-

---

[25] As noted earlier, the sole exception to this was the consultation mechanism established under Article 118 of the Treaty of Rome, which the Commission rarely utilized.

[26] As Callovi (1995) notes, the Commission was reluctant to make proposals pertaining to the abolition of internal controls out of a desire to avoid various legal and philosophical battles. Thus, even in this area of Community competence, the Commission took a back seat to intergovernmental deliberations.

cation thus made clear that the long-term goal of harmonizing the immigration policies of member states was to take a back seat to the more immediate goal of eliminating border controls at intra-community frontiers by 1992.

THE EXPLOSION OF INTEREST IN IMMIGRATION ISSUES

The complexity and sensitivity of issues stemming from the EC's free-movement goals, and their central relationship to questions of both internal and external border controls, resulted in the intensive consideration of immigration and immigration-related issues within a growing number of organizations. Within the European Community, several long-term intergovernmental groups—such as the Trevi, Customs Mutual Assistance Group (MAG), and European Political Cooperation (EPC) groups (see box 3-3, p. 32)—expanded their mandates (most often informally) to deal with immigration issues.[27]

Not surprisingly, the proliferation of institutional mechanisms for considering immigration and asylum issues led to *de facto* overlapping agendas, which in turn led to duplication and conflicts among the various processes, heightened mutual mistrust, and an unwillingness to cooperate. Domestic agency competition within member states compounded these problems, making closure on even the most basic procedural matters difficult.

While such undesirable dynamics in interagency relationships are not unusual when jurisdictions and constituencies overlap, they were augmented in this case by such factors as the reluctance of member states to surrender control over immigration matters and concern that some states would lack the commitment and capacity to implement agreed-upon measures—with potentially disastrous

---

[27] This was also true of several multilateral organizations outside the EC. These include the Informal Intergovernmental Consultations on Asylum, Refugees, and Migration Policies in Europe, North America, and Australia (IGC); the Vienna Group and the Berlin and Budapest Processes (under the auspices of the Council of Europe); and the Conference on Security and Cooperation in Europe (CSCE, now the Organization for Security and Cooperation in Europe [OSCE]). In addition, several organizations with long track records on the study of immigration issues—for example the Organisation for Economic Co-operation and Development (OECD), the International Labour Organization (ILO), and the International Organization for Migration (IOM)—also considerably intensified their immigration work (see box 3-4, p. 34). Sadly, much of the activism and the waning interest in cooperation among many of these organizations on immigration matters can be attributed to institutional desires to stake a place in an obviously up-and-coming policy issue and thus gain an inside track in acquiring the resources that such a policy interest typically entails.

effects on the Community's ability to control access to the region. Countries comfortable with their own border-control mechanisms (e.g., the United Kingdom) perceived Community-wide controls to have many disadvantages. For instance, securing timely changes in administrative policy in order to respond to a new external-border challenge would be more difficult, and removing internal-border controls would ease access to the country by unauthorized persons who might have gained entry into the Community as a result of enforcement failures by another member state.

SEEKING BOTH SECURITY AND A FRONTIER-FREE SPACE

As all eyes appeared focused on the effort to eliminate internal frontiers, the European Council began to recognize that implementation of Article 8a was threatened by inadequate communication and cooperation among the numerous "free movement" groups. Furthermore, newly perceived threats—terrorism, international crime, drug trafficking, and illegal immigration—had grown in importance, leading most member states to conclude that progress in establishing an internal frontier-free space was directly linked to intergovernmental cooperation in combating these new threats.

THE COORDINATORS' GROUP AND THE PALMA DOCUMENT

At its December 1988 meeting in Rhodes, the Council directed each member state to appoint a person responsible for coordinating Community activities relating to the free movement of persons, with the hope of turning "Europe into a tangible reality for its citizens" (Coordinators' Group 1989:1). These individuals would constitute the **Coordinators' Group on the Free Movement of Persons**, which was assigned the ambitious task of achieving congruence among the various positions adopted by each of the intergovernmental fora. Comprised of senior officials from EC member states, with the participation of the Commission, the Coordinators' Group oversaw the often overlapping agendas and activities of the Ad Hoc Immigration Group, the Trevi Group, and Mutual Assistance Group, the Judicial Cooperation Group on European Political Cooperation, and the Horizontal Group on Data Processing.[28]

---

[28] The Coordinators' Group was replaced by the K.4 Committee after the Treaty on European Union entered into force.

31

3-3. INTERGOVERNMENTAL COMMUNITY FORA WITH IMMIGRATION-RELATED MANDATES

The *Trevi Group,* named after the site of the group's first meeting (near the Trevi Fountain in Rome), was formed in 1976 at the request of the U.K. Presidency to coordinate efforts against terrorism. The Trevi Group brings together senior Justice and Interior officials to discuss law enforcement issues. In 1980, its mandate was extended to include issues related to illegal immigration and asylum flows. Its four working groups are: (1) terrorism; (2) police cooperation; (3) serious crimes and drug trafficking (since 1985); and (4) policing and security implications of the Single European Act. The Commission participates in the Trevi Group's activities.

The *Horizontal Group on Data Processing* was created by the Coordinators' Group on the Free Movement of Persons to coordinate the processing of data exchanged among member states. The Horizontal Group's principal function was to establish the **European Information System (EIS)**. Like the Schengen Information System, the European Information System is designed to combat more serious forms of crime, as well as to strengthen external border controls and police cooperation in fighting illegal immigration networks. It will also link the information systems of member states to a central database and has raised similar concerns about privacy and accuracy. As with the Schengen countries, error-free operation of the EIS is viewed as a prerequisite to the creation of a frontier-free space among EU member states. At its June 1992 meeting in Lisbon, the Council requested that a convention be drafted to operationalize the EIS. Though responsibility for its establishment initially fell to the Trevi Group, the EIS has since been developed in collaboration with the Horizontal Group on Data Processing.

The *Customs Mutual Assistance Group (MAG)* was established in 1989 to focus on customs and other technical information-exchange and maintenance issues in order to strengthen and coordinate customs checks at external borders. As part of the effort to develop a computerized customs information-exchange system, MAG proposed a solution known as the **System for Customs Enforcement Network (SCENT)**, which would have enabled national customs services to exchange limited information beginning in 1992. However, on November 22, 1992, the "Convention between the Member States of the European Economic Community Concerning the Use of Information Technology for Customs Purposes" was finalized and approved by the European Council, thereby eliminating the need for SCENT.

The *European Committee to Combat Drugs (CELAD)* was created in 1989 to bridge gaps in and better coordinate member states' national policies on narcotics. CELAD's work led to the adoption by the European Council in December 1990 of the First European Plan to Combat Drugs and to a revised and updated version two years later. CELAD's work also led to the adoption by the Council of a Regulation for the Creation of the European Monitoring Center for Drugs and Drug Addiction.

The *European Political Cooperation Group (EPC)*, created in October 1970 as a forum for regularizing the meetings of member states' Foreign Ministers, was the result of a desire to establish a harmonized approach to Community foreign policy. Though immigration has yet to come under the Community's foreign policy agenda, the EPC's work corresponds to a number of border-related matters, such as drug trafficking and judicial cooperation on civil and penal matters.

Sources: Coordinators' Group 1991b and Cruz 1993.

3-4. RELATED INTERNATIONAL (NON–EC/EU) FORA

The *Council of Europe (COE)* is one of the more important organizations addressing migration in Europe. The COE provides the institutional framework for a number of immigration and asylum sub-groups; although it lacks an institutional mechanism within the EU to enforce compliance with its resolutions, the COE's meetings on migration-related matters carry substantial *political* weight. The COE's European Social Charter (1961), which aims to protect the social rights of migrants, and its 1977 Convention on the Legal Status of Migrant Workers, which recognizes an extensive set of social and economic rights for migrants and their families, do carry a significant amount of moral suasion and, in a way, often set the tone and agenda for political activists and "Europeanists" in various national governments.

Australia, Canada, and the United States join COE members as observers in its twice-a-year meetings. Until its responsibilities were assumed by the EC's Ad Hoc Immigration Group (AHIG), the COE's Committee of Experts on the Legal Aspects of Territorial Asylum, Refugees, and Stateless People (CAHAR), the oldest European body dealing with asylum issues, was the principal vehicle for the discussion of a European convention on the country of first asylum. After two unsuccessful attempts to achieve signature of such a convention in 1987 and 1988, these efforts were abandoned, and EC members instead shifted their attention to drafting the Dublin Convention (and its extension to Central Europe, the EFTA countries, and Canada through the parallel agreements).

The *Vienna Group* was one of several bodies formed as a result of a conference organized by the Council of Europe on the "Movement of Persons from Central and East European Countries" held in Vienna in January 1991 in response to shared concerns over potential mass migrations from the East. The conference included the senior immigration officials of 35 sending and receiving countries, and focused on the " . . . positive steps [needed] to prevent the emigration of those Eastern European nationals most able to assist in the economic and cultural development of their homelands." The officials also noted the inability of EC labor markets to support an increase in immigration. They recommended vigilant efforts to prevent conditions that might result in an uncontrolled influx of migrants; common measures against illegal immigration; the exchange of information on labor market conditions within Central and Eastern European states; and implementation of technical assistance and vocational training and exchange programs to promote development and prevent emigration. With respect to asylum, the officials agreed that they would try to harmonize regional asylum policies in compliance with the 1951 Geneva Convention relating to the Status of Refugees. The *Vienna Group* held five subsequent meetings to look into the recommendations adopted at the 1991 conference.

The 1991 Conference also established the **Ad Hoc Committee of experts for identity documents and the movement of persons (CAHID)** to follow up on its recommendations. A separate though related group, the **Vienna Club**, has brought together Justice and Interior Ministers of Austria, France, Germany, Italy, and Switzerland every two years since the 1991 Conference to discuss border issues related to immigration and asylum.

In October 1991, at the initiative of the German Interior Minister, a conference consisting of Vienna Club members, non-Club EC member states, and 13 Eastern and Central European states was convened in Berlin to discuss clandestine immigration from the East. As in the case of the Vienna Conference, a **Berlin Group** was established to look into the recommendations of the Berlin Conference. At their third meeting on January 12-13, 1993, in Bonn, the Group drafted new recommendations aimed at preventing illegal immigration, including criminal penalties and sanctions for alien smuggling, cooperation to counter the penetration of illegal immigration networks, enhanced border checks and surveillance, and re-entry criteria.

At the February 15-16, 1993 Budapest meeting of the Berlin Group, participants discussed these recommendations and agreed to meet again as the **Budapest Group**. The Budapest Group was comprised of representatives of those states assuming the presidencies of the EC, the parties to the Schengen Agreement, the member states of the EFTA, the Czech Republic, the Slovak Republic, Poland, and Hungary.

Europe, the United States, Canada, and Australia meet as part of the informal **Intergovernmental Consultations on Asylum, Refugees and Migration Policies in Europe, North America and Australia (IGC)**,[a] based in Geneva, to discuss issues of common concern, primarily with respect to asylum. The IGC is an informal forum for exchanging views and experiences; it is co-sponsored by the U.N. High Commissioner for Refugees and the International Organization of Migration. The IGC's agenda and non-binding reports are developed on the basis of membership interest.

The **Organization for Security and Cooperation in Europe (OSCE)** (formerly the Conference on Security and Cooperation in Europe [CSCE]) has assumed a distinct role on human and minority rights issues that are at the heart of ethnic conflict. Such conflict is widely understood to have significant migration and asylum consequences. The OSCE is the forum in which the countries of Eastern Europe and the Commonwealth of Independent States meet with the advanced industrial democracies to discuss such issues. The OSCE's Office for Democratic Institutions and Human Rights is responsible for these matters, while the Organization's High Commissioner on National Minorities advocates in behalf of minority rights. The OSCE places great value on the participation of nongovernmental actors.

3-4. continued

The *Organisation for Economic Co-operation and Development (OECD)* boasts more than twenty years of commitment to the study of labor market aspects of migration; it has sponsored three significant international conferences since 1991 (in Rome, Madrid, and Tokyo). The Migration Working Party is the OECD's relevant organization on this issue. The Working Party serves as a forum for OECD members to exchange information on national policies and practices and to discuss matters related to migration, with emphasis on labor market and other economic and social aspects. It systematically collects, reviews, and disseminates information, using the Continuous Reporting System on Migration (SOPEMI), as well as statistical data and information on policies and practices of members countries and, to the extent feasible, of relevant non-member countries. The Working Party also analyzes the economic, demographic, and social causes and consequences of migration in sending and receiving countries and their wide-ranging policy implications. It evaluates and develops (on the basis of analytical work) policy options that would facilitate decisions by OECD members to respond to the challenges and opportunities of international migration, including the integration and reintegration of migrants and their children in the economy and society at large. Finally, the Working Party encourages and facilitates cooperation among sending and receiving countries by providing information and policy analysis to assist them in assessing and managing migration flows to their mutual benefit. The OECD's annual publication, *Trends in International Migration*, is a standard reference work in this area.

The *International Labor Organization (ILO)*, a specialized agency of the United Nations, has a long-standing interest in matters concerning the labor rights of migrant workers and their families.

In addition to extensive programmatic responsibilities on international migration, the *International Organization of Migration (IOM)* convenes conferences and seminars addressing a variety of migration-related topics. Since 1991, the IOM has devoted particular attention to Eastern Europe and the former Soviet Union. The IOM's main publication, *International Migration*, is a leading publication in the field.

Sources: Cruz 1993 and Council of Europe 1991a.

[a] Not to be confused with the Intergovernmental Conferences (IGCs) convened by EC member states to prepare amendments to the Treaty of Rome.

The Coordinators' authority stemmed partly from the Group's intergovernmental composition (which allowed member governments, rather than the Commission, to be in control) and partly from the body's unambiguous terms of reference. Specifically, the Group was charged with "coordinating, giving an impetus to, and unblocking the whole complex of intergovernmental and Community work in the field of the free movement of persons" (Ibid.:3).

The Coordinators' first assignment was to prepare a report on measures necessary for creating an area without internal frontiers. The **Free Movement of Persons Report**, which came to be known as the **Palma Document** after the Coordinators approved it in Palma de Mallorca, Spain, was adopted by the European Council at its June 1989 meeting in Madrid. Considered the Community's internal-frontier-elimination master plan, the Palma Document outlined a dual strategy of first strengthening checks at the Community's external frontiers and then abolishing internal borders.

Within each of these components, measures considered to be of high priority were listed as "essential."[29] Other provisions were listed as "desirable" and could be implemented whenever possible. Measures to strengthen external frontiers included the establishment of a common visa policy[30] and a common refugee and asylum policy.[31] Internal provisions included, among other things,

---

[29] "Essential" external border measures included the definition of checks and surveillance at external frontiers (by 1990), improved cooperation among law enforcement and customs agencies (by 1991), information-exchanges on "wanted" or "inadmissable" persons (by the end of 1990), efforts to combat illegal immigration networks, and the solution to problems stemming from bilateral relations with third countries (both before January 1, 1993). Internal frontier measures considered essential included a study on the abolition of checks on TCNs (by the end of 1989), concluding agreements pertaining to the readmission of TCNs (by the end of 1990), and cooperation among law enforcement and customs agencies (Coordinators' Group 1989 [Annex I]:4-7).

[30] A common list of countries whose nationals would require a visa to enter EC space (to be updated every six months), and harmonization of criteria and procedures for granting visas constituted the "essential" visa measures. The creation of a common visa application (by the end of 1989), a common "European visa" (by the end of 1992), and the computerization of information-exchanges on visa procedures (by the end of 1991) were only deemed "desirable" (Coordinators' Group 1989 [Annex I]:11).

[31] Among the priority measures in this area were the drafting and entry into force of a convention determining the state responsible for examining asylum claims, the specification of asylee and refugee movement in Community space (by 1992), a streamlined procedure for processing "unfounded" applications (by the end of 1989), and the acceptance of identical international agreements with respect to asylum (1992). In contrast, agreement on common criteria for the granting of asylum or refugee status was considered "desirable" (by the first half of 1990) (Coordinators' Group 1989 [Annex I]:12).

measures to combat terrorism, drug trafficking, and other illegal trafficking, as well as measures to improve law enforcement cooperation and judicial cooperation.

The Palma Document identified the responsible fora and targeted dates for implementing the various measures. The Coordinators' Group was charged with coordinating the activities of these fora to ensure completion by the agreed dates. Attaining even modest levels of coordination, however, proved elusive. Moreover, the seemingly endless emergence of new challenges, such as those posed by the collapsing Soviet bloc,[32] presented additional obstacles to coordination while simultaneously creating an even greater need for it.

For those eager to point to (or patient enough to search for) signs of discernible progress on the integration front, there was usually something tangible enough to allow for a certain amount of optimism, or at least to make those impatient with the slow pace of *substantial* progress toward policy harmonization appear unduly pessimistic. For instance, at the December 1989 Strasbourg Summit, the heads of eleven member states (with the United Kingdom abstaining) adopted a **Community Charter of the fundamental social rights of workers**, in which they acknowledged the importance of guaranteeing legally resident TCNs social and economic rights "comparable" to those of Community nationals (Commission 1990a:10). Nevertheless, by the end of the 1980s, it was clear that little progress could be expected on either equal treatment for TCNs or their movement within EC territory.

Indeed, measurable substantive (as opposed to procedural) progress toward formal policy harmonization has been rare—even among like-minded states. If anything, one detects a retreat even from intergovernmental principles, as most EC member states have reasserted national prerogatives. This "retreat" is evident despite an *ad nauseam* pattern of statements committing ". . . to preserve the open attitudes of [member] States towards the rest of the

---

32 On December 8 and 9, 1989—one month after the fall of the Berlin Wall—an alarmed Council noted that ". . . the progressive abolition of [internal] border formalities shall not affect the right of member states to take such measures as they consider necessary for the purpose of controlling immigration from third countries" (Council 1989:10). A few days later in Paris, the Immigration Ministers resolved to ". . . adapt their policies as required, in order to respond to those developments " while simultaneously agreeing to lift visa requirements for East Germans (see AHIG 1991a:20).

world" and to "uphold the rights and safeguards of foreigners whose presence [in any member state] is valid" (AHIG 1991a:97). Optimistic rhetoric such as this typically suggested far greater progress than had been or realistically could be achieved, given the sovereignty-impinging nature of immigration initiatives.

THE DUBLIN CONVENTION ON ASYLUM

In forging ahead with the Palma Document's proposed agenda and timetable, eleven EC member states signed the so-called **Dublin Convention** on June 15, 1990.[33] Denmark signed the Convention the following year. By determining which state was responsible for handling an asylum claim, the Convention sought to prevent the filing of multiple or consecutive claims by the same individual in EC space. It also intended to prevent the problem of the "refugee in orbit," which can occur if no state accepts responsibility for adjudicating an asylum claim (AHIG 1991a:65) (see box **3-5**, p. 41).

Success in negotiating the Dublin Convention has not, however, been mirrored by corresponding ease in its ratification. As of this writing, only ten of the twelve signatories have ratified the Convention.[34] A combination of the culture of secrecy that permeates EC/EU deliberations (energizing those who opposed the measure), numerous legal challenges, and concerns over the absence of legal recourse at the Community level for rejected asylum claimants has prevented the Convention from coming into effect.

PUBLIC ORDER AND SECURITY CONCERNS

While the rhetoric of progress toward implementing the goals of Article 8a continued to outpace performance by large margins, growing concern over potential influxes from Central and Eastern Europe became the catalyst for sustained, increasingly systematic discussion about external border controls. Here there was consid-

---

[33] The full name of the Convention is the **Convention Determining the State Responsible for Examining Applications for Asylum Lodged in One of the Member States of the European Communities**. The Ad Hoc Immigration Group incorporated the asylum provisions of the Schengen Supplementary Convention, which was also signed in June 1990, as the basis of complementary measures in the Dublin Convention (Bunyan and Webber 1995:24).

[34] The Dutch Senate is considering but has not yet approved ratification of the Convention. The Irish parliamentary procedures for ratification have not yet begun.

erable room for gains in policy cooperation, since member states shared similar security concerns, particularly over the potential for uncontrolled movement of criminals, terrorists, and drugs that might accompany the creation of a frontier-free space.

As the focus of the discussion shifted steadily toward controls, the issue became thematically linked ever more closely with the priorities of the Trevi Group—the ministers responsible for public order and security (see box **3-3**, p. 32). One of the Trevi Group's foci was the Community's eastern neighbors. While Western Europeans were initially inspired by the collapse of the former Soviet bloc, enthusiasm and altruism quickly gave way to concern over the potential for massive migrations from the East.[35] Fearing the establishment of a "single market in crime," the Trevi Group, meeting in Dublin in June 1990, agreed on a program that would focus on "reinforcing" and "building [on] . . . existing cooperation in the fight against terrorism, drug trafficking, organized crime and illegal immigration" (Trevi Group 1990:3).[36] The program further recognized that success in these efforts would require increased information exchanges about criminal activities; intensified oversight of external land, sea, and air frontiers; and improved cooperation at common frontiers (Ibid.).

The Trevi ministers had good reason to be optimistic that their program would develop apace. Even before 1990, relevant proposals for cooperation were in varying stages of development. These included: (a) a European Central Drugs Intelligence Unit (EDIU) and a European Common Information System (EIS); (b) a French proposal to provide training for law enforcement officers from drug-producing and transit countries; and (c) an Irish proposal to develop liaison services both for the exchange of information with Eastern European states and for technical assistance to help those states reorganize and develop their police services in order to combat terrorism throughout Europe.

---

[35] No country felt these concerns more directly or intensely than Germany, which in 1989 had received approximately half a million newcomers. Of these, close to 350,000 were East Germans who had crossed into West Germany, and about 120,000 were asylum seekers. As the Community's easternmost member, Germany clearly had the most to lose from instability in countries beyond its eastern frontiers.

[36] Many of these agenda items had been advanced in the Palma Document to offset measures stemming from the abolition of internal frontiers.

3-5. THE DUBLIN CONVENTION[a]

The *Convention Determining the State Responsible for Examining Applications for Asylum Lodged in One of the Member States of the European Communities, or the "Dublin Convention,"* was signed in Dublin on June 15, 1990 by 11 European Community member states and by Denmark the following year. The Convention aims to avoid multiple applications for asylum while at the same time guaranteeing that an asylum request is examined by one of the member states.

The Convention sets out several criteria for determining which state is responsible for examining asylum applications. The order of responsibility is set out as follows: (1) the state where the applicant has a close family member with recognized refugee status within the meaning of the 1951 Geneva Convention; (2) the state issuing a residence permit or entry visa, or if more than one, the state issuing the permit or visa with the longest validity or the latest expiration date; (3) if a transit visa was issued, the responsibility will rest with either the destination state or the state where the application is lodged, depending on the particular circumstances; (4) in cases of demonstrable illegal entry, the first entry state will usually be responsible unless an asylum application is made in another state where the applicant stayed for longer than six months; (5) in cases of legal entry, the state that waived the requirement for a visa will usually be responsible. If none of the above criteria apply, the state where the application is lodged will be responsible.

In addition, the Convention sets up obligations and procedures regarding the transfer or taking back of the applicant between states, and requires information exchange on national legislation, regulatory measures or practices in the field of asylum, statistical data, general information on trends, and individual cases. (The Council of Ministers has set up CIREA in compliance with this provision; see box **4-2**, p. 70-71). Nothing in the Convention interferes with a signatory's right to send applicants back to a third state that is not a member of the European Union.

The Dublin Convention also establishes strict time limits for determining which state is responsible for examining an asylum application.

---

[a] Not to be confused with the **Dublin Group**, a group of 41 countries (including EU member states, the United States, and Japan) that have met since 1991 to discuss drug and drug-related activities. This Group is serviced by the EU Council Secretariat.

3-5. continued

For example, according to Article 11 of the Convention, if within six months a state does not request another state to take charge of an asylum application for which it is responsible, responsibility will rest with the state in which the application was lodged. If a state that has been requested to take responsibility for an application does not act on the request within three months of the receipt of the claim, it is in effect accepting the claim. Article 11 further stipulates that "[t]ransfer of the [asylum] applicant . . . from the member state where the application was lodged to the member state responsible must take place not later than one month after acceptance of the request to take charge [of the application] or one month after the conclusion of any proceedings initiated by the alien challenging the transfer decision . . ." (Another example of the strict time limit is Article 13 of the Convention, which requires member states to respond to an application to take back an asylum applicant within eight days of its submission.)

The ongoing work for implementing the Dublin Convention falls under the third pillar (intergovernmental cooperation on Justice and Home Affairs) of the European Union and is subject to its procedures and structures. Once the Convention is in force, a committee consisting of a representative from each state and chaired by the member state holding the Presidency of the Council will be established. The committee will examine questions of a general nature concerning the application and interpretation of the Convention and may set up working parties.

A principal obstacle to implementing the Dublin Convention has been the unwillingness of its signatories to endorse each others' legal and regulatory asylum adjudication mechanisms out of concern that such endorsement might dilute individual countries' national humanitarian protection standards. Adherence to the Convention could also raise fundamental constitutional and international legal issues for states that have signed prior refugee protection and human rights accords. Legal challenges and concerns over the absence of legal recourse at the Community level for rejected asylum claimants have also prevented the Convention from coming into effect.

As of December 1995, ten of the twelve EU members (i.e., not including Ireland and the Netherlands) had ratified the Convention; the three accession countries (Austria, Finland, and Sweden) were in various stages of ratification. Only the Netherlands may eventually prove to be an insurmountable obstacle to implementation, in that the Dutch Parliament has insisted that the European Court of Justice be given *full* competence in matters pertaining to the Convention as a condition for its ratification.

PARALLEL DUBLIN CONVENTION

On February 3-4, 1992, a parallel convention to the Dublin Convention was drafted for the EFTA countries (Austria, Sweden, Norway, Finland, Iceland, Switzerland, and Liechtenstein) and Canada. However, formal negotiations and/or agreements on the parallel convention are legally contingent on ratification of the Dublin Convention by all EU member states and on the resolution of a number of substantive and procedural questions pertaining to the Treaty on European Union. As a result, on May 8, 1992—and notwithstanding the fact that the AHIG's Subgroup on Asylum had already reached agreement on the draft parallel convention—the Ad Hoc Immigration Group decided ". . . not to pursue the idea of concluding an additional protocol to the Dublin Convention . . . with third countries."

There were two major sticking points. The first pertained to the TEU requirement that the authority for such negotiations rest with the K.4 Committee, which had not yet been created. The second impediment stemmed from the Dublin Convention's Article 22, which stipulates that signatories should have ratified the European Convention for the Protection of Human Rights and Fundamental Freedoms, the Geneva Convention relating to the Status of Refugees, and the New York Protocol. Not all states interested in joining a parallel convention meet these conditions.

Sources: AHIG 1992a and European Communities 1990.

DRAFT CONVENTION ON THE CROSSING OF EXTERNAL FRONTIERS

This was the broader environment in which the Coordinators' Group sought to push forward with implementation of Article 8a. The primary emphasis of the Group's second report, submitted to the Dublin Council on June 17, 1990, was a draft **Convention on the Crossing of External Frontiers** (hereafter, **External Frontiers Convention, or EFC**). This document defined the concept of external borders and stipulated the conditions for crossing them. It also outlined the conditions under which third-country nationals residing in one EC country could travel to another without a visa, thus signaling the first, albeit tentative, EC-wide[37] step toward the development of a frontier-free space for TCNs residing within the Community (see box **3-6**, pp. 46-47). It did not, however, extend to TCNs the right to settle anywhere in Community space—a prerequisite, in the view of many Commissioners and member state officials, to establishing an area that is truly without internal frontiers.

The Coordinators also reported that privacy concerns[38] raised by the proposed European Information System (EIS) pertaining to the use of personalized data banks had been worked out, and that a draft Convention on the EIS was ready for signature. They further urged greater consultations and cooperation in the field of immigration, and made note of the need to keep the public better informed of the work under way to achieve the goals of Article 8a. Although obtaining popular support is essential for any effort requiring significant coordination across states, this last point was, and often continues to be, grossly undervalued, if not ignored.

A DUAL-TRACK APPROACH: CONTROLS AND INTEGRATION

At the December 1990 Summit in Rome, the Coordinators submitted two reports to the Council based on an inventory of member states' immigration and asylum positions. The reports, which had been commissioned by the Strasbourg Council the previous December, consisted of two separate evaluations.

---

[37] On a smaller regional scale, the Schengen Agreement—the *de facto* blueprint for the External Frontiers Convention—listed similar goals.

[38] These concerns stemmed from the fact that personal information on EU citizens would be stored in these data banks and that a central bureaucracy would be able to track the movement of persons in EC territory. The Schengen Information System, for instance—a smaller version of the EIS—would have information on up to 1.5 million EU citizens stored in its central data base.

The first, prepared by a group of independent experts appointed by the Commission, considered the issue of integrating immigrants in member countries. It also discussed immigration controls, but stressed that the "main pillars of an immigration policy" must include "the granting of permanent residence, equal opportunities in jobs, education, vocational training and housing, easier access to naturalization, and tolerance between communities especially by the establishment of structures for dialogue" (Commission 1990b:1).

The second report, prepared by the Ad Hoc Immigration Group focused on the conditions under which TCNs could enter and move within member states. Noting that the EC was under increasing pressure to admit migrants from Eastern Europe and the South, it concluded that the "control of migratory flows [was] an especially important aspect of policy on the integration of immigrants" (Coordinators' Group 1990b:2).

These parallel reports highlighted what had become the essence of the Community's, and later the Union's (as well as that of several individual members states) approach to immigration: the need to restrict further immigration in order to better integrate TCNs already residing permanently in EC space. Both reports also stressed the crucial point—strenuously resisted by some—that (except for Ireland) member states had become important countries of immigration. Not surprisingly, the Coordinators called for joint efforts to: (a) control pressures for new admission and (b) facilitate the social and labor market integration of legally present TCNs and their families.

The Coordinators also underscored the importance of continuing to observe the principle of family reunification, while urging greater coordination on asylum issues with a view toward eventual policy harmonization. On asylum—one of the Community's most troubling social, political, and increasingly, economic issues in the 1990s—they urged full cooperation with the U.N. High Commissioner for Refugees (UNHCR) to comply with the principles set forth in the 1951 Geneva Convention relating to the Status of Refugees, as amended by the 1967 New York Protocol. They also recommended that member states extend aid and trade incentives to countries of emigration in order to alleviate some of the economic causes of migration (Ibid.:6). This was an early reference to what was later termed a "root causes" approach—the first time the linkage was made so forcefully—although the Coordina-

3-6. EXTERNAL FRONTIERS CONVENTION

The discussion of external border controls arose out of concern about the burden of responsibility that member states with long external land or sea borders would be forced to bear in protecting the Community's external frontiers. At their Munich meeting in June 1988, the Immigration Ministers asked the AHIG to draw up a questionnaire identifying measures that member states felt were necessary to ensure control of the Community's external frontiers. The conclusions were presented at the December 1988 ministerial meeting in Athens, after which the AHIG was instructed to develop proposals for external border controls to be carried out after January 1, 1993. These proposals, presented at the Madrid meeting in May 1989, marked the beginning of the drafting of the External Frontiers Convention. At their Paris meeting in December 1989, the Ministers instructed that work on the Convention be completed no later than 1990.

Following the program approved by the Madrid Council in connection with the Dublin Convention (see box **3-5**, pp. 41-43), member states began to work at the intergovernmental level on drafting a *"Convention on Crossings at the External Frontiers of the Member States,"* or *"External Frontiers Convention."* This work was conducted under the authority of the Ministers Responsible for Immigration, and resulted in an agreement in June 1991 on a set of principles that were to be given formal shape in a convention.

The proposed convention defines external borders as (a) a member state's land frontier which is not contiguous with a frontier of another member state, and maritime frontiers; and (b) airports and seaports, "except where they are considered to be internal frontiers for purposes of instruments enacted under the Treaty establishing the EC." The draft convention also outlines the conditions under which third-country nationals residing in one EC member state can travel to another. It prohibits TCNs from working in the country they are visiting and from staying longer than three months.

After nearly five years of negotiations, the Immigration Ministers were unable to reach agreement on all of the principles forming the basis of the External Frontiers Convention. Though intended for signature at the end of the Luxembourg Presidency in June 1991, the text was—and continues to be—held up over a number of disputes, most notably that between the United Kingdom and Spain over **Gibraltar**. Spain feels that it should have a say in controlling persons entering the EC through Gibraltar, while the United Kingdom and other member states argue that the border between Spain and Gibraltar is an internal frontier that should not be subject to the External Frontiers Convention. An additional obstacle is the United Kingdom's growing insistence that disputes arising from Community conventions remain outside the competence of the European Court of Justice.

Failure to resolve the issues surrounding the convention has dealt a severe blow to the decision-making sequence outlined in the Palma Document. Following agreement on the External Frontiers and European Information System Conventions, member states were supposed to shift their focus to the abolition of internal frontier controls. In the absence of closure on these conventions, the goal of creating internal-border-free space remains unattainable.

On December 19, 1993, the Commission issued a proposal calling for a Council Decision to establish a *Convention on Controls on Persons Crossing External Frontiers*. The revised convention sought to salvage the principles in the EFC that had already been agreed upon by member states, while incorporating the changes that had become necessary as a consequence of the entry into force of the TEU. As of the end of 1995, the revised draft convention had yet to be signed.

Sources: AHIG 1991a and Commission 1993c.

tors acknowledged that the limited resources available for aid made it an insufficient supplement to immigration policies.

With unusual clarity and directness, the Coordinators also stressed the need for policy harmonization, although they simultaneously acknowledged its unlikelihood. They stated that although member states considered immigration policy to be an area of sovereign responsibility, they needed to consider the "*European* dimension" when devising and implementing such policies. Nevertheless, the Coordinators added, "since Member States' demographic and economic situations [were] very often different and some Member States [had] historic links with third countries, this European dimension [could] only take the form of co-ordination in the short and medium term, [although in] the long term a greater degree of harmonization of immigration policies could be sought" (Ibid.:3).

The Coordinators' reports reflected their growing authority as well as the evolution of Commission and member-state thinking on both controls and integration; in both areas, the Coordinators made more specific recommendations than previously. On the control front, for instance, they called for adoption of the recently drafted External Frontiers Convention and recommended concrete measures to combat illegal immigration and residence. These proposals focused on targeting the channels and individuals that facilitated unlawful entry, the unauthorized employment of foreigners, visa overstays, checks to detect illegal residents, and the repatriation of unauthorized residents. Similarly, on immigrant integration, the Coordinators discussed the employment, residence, and social rights of legally resident TCNs in the context of larger EC-wide deliberations on preferential treatment in the hiring of Community nationals. They also considered ways in which the international commitments of the member states and the Community affected such rights.[39]

---

[39] In contrast to the Commission, member states have attached lower priority to matters regarding the employment rights of TCNs. The first time that a Council Presidency even chose to broach that topic publicly—albeit quite gingerly and with a pronounced protectionist slant—was on October 22, 1992. At that time, the U.K. Presidency submitted a draft resolution for adoption by EC Immigration (and Employment) Ministers, addressing the harmonization of national policies on the admission for employment of non-EC nationals to the territories of the member states. The Ministers resolved that strict controls should be maintained and that member states' national policies should adhere to a set of principles that would not be specified until mid-1994. The resolution also required that all national legislation on TCN employment be revised to conform with these principles by January 1, 1996 (see AHIG 1992f).

IMPLEMENTING ARTICLE 8A

While the Coordinators' early work on implementing Article 8a appeared to be remarkably focused and thoughtful, if overly ambitious, it was not particularly politically persuasive when measured in terms of Council receptivity to its recommendations. The Rome Council (December 1990), for instance, took no action on the Coordinators' recommendations for implementing the 1989 Palma Document. It merely noted "with regret" the delays in achieving the provisions on the free movement of persons and urged that "the necessary decisions" regarding the crossing of external borders be taken as soon as possible in order to meet the January 1, 1993, deadline for the removal of internal frontiers (Coordinators' Group 1991a:2).

Subsequent Councils have been equally long on "preambular" and hortatory language, but short on action on these matters. Thus, at the June 1991 Luxembourg Summit, the Coordinators proposed an ambitious policy agenda that included such fundamental and still unresolved issues as (a) the speedy ratification of the Dublin Convention; (b) the developmental and management matters associated with the "Troika's" rapid-consultation center for dealing with sudden large-scale migrations[40]; and (c) the creation of a privacy-sensitive data-processing system for storing information on the activities of the AHIG, the Trevi Group, and the Customs Mutual Assistance Group. The Coordinators also urged that action be completed on establishing the European Information System, external border checks, cross-border police cooperation, the right of cross-border pursuit and observation, and the development of the European Drugs Unit (Ibid.:4-6).[41] Despite the Coordinators' considerable activism, the Council again did little to implement the recommendations.

---

[40] The "Troika" is composed of the previous, current, and upcoming EC/EU presidencies; it is intended to ensure policy and management continuity within the Council despite the biannual rotations of the presidency. The rapid consultation center has not been successful. It has held only one meeting at the ministerial level—in September of 1991, to deal with the influx of Albanians to Italy.

[41] The Coordinators' Group further informed the Council of the status of its study on customs enforcement, noting that an enforcement strategy had been endorsed by all Community heads of customs services. It also noted that *conditional* agreement had been reached on a new Protocol to the 1967 Naples Convention on the Provision of Mutual Assistance by Customs Authorities of EC Member States, covering such issues as national coordination services, liaison officers, cross-border surveillance and pursuit, and cooperation relating to the disposition of proceeds from illicit drug trafficking (Coordinators' Group 1991b:5-6).

A frequently overlooked impediment to the Coordinators' progress may have been their own ambivalence about the viability of full freedom of movement goals. Such underlying ambivalence frustrates the results-oriented analyst. On one level, one detects a clearer and more direct affirmation of basic principles, apparent gains in momentum, definite gains in productivity, and much more integrated thinking across the full array of Article 8a issues—in sum, a certain dynamism that typically sets the stage for real progress. On another level, one continues to observe lack of closure on several critical issues—a function, perhaps, of the member states' (and the entire advanced industrial world's) intensifying political, social, and cultural introspection. Indeed, it seems clear that EC member states were simply not yet willing to commit to tangible forms of coordination.

It is, however, possible to set the threshold too high in any analytical exercise that focuses more on outcomes than on process. Doing so tends to overshadow the fact that palpable progress *was* being made—although it was evolutionary rather than revolutionary.[42] In such a framework, one cannot always perceive when the next step in a process has been attained. The real question, then, becomes whether small changes were creating enough momentum to change the Community's posture from one of *status quo*-based inertia to one of measurable, dynamic progress.

THE INTERGOVERNMENTAL CONFERENCE OF 1991 AND THE SEARCH FOR A COMMON IMMIGRATION POLICY

By the end of 1990, inertia was much more evident than progress—with any dynamism coming from the maneuvering between those member states that argued for gradual but limited

---

[42] For example, the Trevi Group made gains through a series of small steps which had the potential for significant forward movement once the political will was summoned—or when momentum itself made significant change inevitable. By mid-1991, Trevi had made progress on such "mundane," though important, law enforcement areas as the training of police personnel, cooperation in forensic police matters, and the posting of liaison officers within and outside the European Community. Less headway had been made on issues relating to the purpose, operation, and future headquarters of the European Drugs Unit—a structure deemed essential by the Interior and Justice Ministers. On civil matters, Trevi Group discussions engaged the issues of adoptions and minor "runaways." And, on criminal matters, the Trevi Group focused on such issues as the application of the 1988 United Nations Convention on money laundering and illicit drug trafficking, which had a June 30, 1991, ratification deadline (see Coordinators' Group 1991b:7-9).

change, and those that sought to push the integration agenda forward through significant revision of the Community's institutional structure. The Intergovernmental Conference on Political Union, launched at the December 1990 Rome Summit,[43] became the forum for vetting these competing visions of Europe. On the one hand, the expected elimination of barriers to the free movement of goods and services by the end of 1992 fueled aspirations for even broader European integration, including free movement of persons. On the other hand, the EC's overlapping and inefficient intergovernmental structures, and the almost pathological secrecy of their deliberations, had become targets of intensifying criticism. The solution proposed by the European Parliament (EP), the Commission, and some member states was to bring these structures into the Community's institutional framework. Such action, it was thought, would make them more efficient and accountable. Specific proposals included subjecting Community decisions to the scrutiny of the Parliament (the Community's only democratically elected body) and granting the European Court of Justice the authority to arbitrate disputes stemming from the application of Community decisions (see Hix 1995:9).

The ensuing and by now familiar debate over whether to address matters *intergovernmentally* (through cooperation, coordination, and the elaboration of conventions) or *supranationally* (through Community law, and thus through extending the competence of the EC's central institutions) posed the greatest obstacle to progress on immigration and other policy matters. Proponents of the intergovernmental route—particularly (but often not only) the United Kingdom and Denmark, which tend to believe that their policies and procedures are both adequate and superior to any that Brussels might develop—have engaged in endless "sovereignty wars" with the Commission. Some countries, including France and the United Kingdom, have expressed concerns about the effects of Community-set policies on their bilateral obligations—and, more broadly, on their ability to act unilaterally. Proponents of the supranational route (most consistently Germany, the Benelux countries, and Italy) are more ideologically pro-Europe; in addition, they have typically calculated that, by allowing the Com-

---

[43] In addition to the IGC on political union, a second Intergovernmental Conference on Economic and Monetary Union was inaugurated at the Summit.

munity to lead, they can blame Brussels for politically unpopular—yet necessary—policies on immigration.[44]

These conflicting views grew more pronounced in the months before the Maastricht Summit. Some member states—particularly Denmark, the United Kingdom, Ireland, and Greece—hoped for far less radical amendments to the Treaty of Rome than those supported by the Commission and the Benelux countries, preferring instead to continue cooperation through the existing intergovernmental structure. Germany struck a middle position, preferring that the Treaty on European Union specify the decision-making arrangements to be used in each policy field prior to their eventual integration into the Community's competence.[45]

LUXEMBOURG VERSUS DUTCH DRAFT TREATIES

In April 1991, the Luxembourg Presidency submitted a draft treaty (also referred to as the **Luxembourg "non-paper"**) proposing a compromise structure for the new Union. In this plan, two intergovernmental "pillars"—one for Common Foreign and Security Policy (CFSP) the other for cooperation in Justice and Home Affairs (JHA)—would co-exist *alongside* the pillar of Community competence, with the Council providing the institutional umbrella connecting the three pillars. Within this so-called "temple" architecture, immigration matters would come under the intergovernmental competence of the Justice and Home Affairs third pillar, and thus remain outside the institutional and jurisdictional framework of the central, Community institutions (Council 1991:10).

At the June 1991 Luxembourg Summit, however, German Chancellor Helmut Kohl called for the adoption of a common immigration policy that would allow for *EC supervision* of the movement of persons once internal borders were removed at the end of 1992.[46] The Council then invited Immigration Ministers to

---

[44] This tactic probably worked better prior to 1991, when the climate was more favorable to Community-led initiatives, but less so thereafter, when Community processes and institutions lost legitimacy.

[45] France also shared a middle position, although its proposed timeframe and scope for integration was slower and more superficial than that of Germany. For a more complete discussion of the various options considered for revising the Treaty of Rome under the Luxembourg Presidency see Hix (1995:9-10).

[46] It is not surprising that Germany, feeling inundated with hundreds of thousands of asylum claims, was instrumental in pushing for the development of Community immigration and asylum policies.

submit proposals on asylum and immigration to the December 1991 Maastricht Council, which was to address, among other things, the possibility of establishing a more comprehensive immigration policy.

For Europe's pro-federalist voices, it was clear that the treaty drafted in April did not go far enough in meeting their ambitions for a united Europe. After assuming the Presidency in July 1991, the Netherlands proceeded to table an alternate draft that sought to bring the intergovernmental policy areas under the competence of the Community's central institutions. Rather than three co-existing pillars, this so-called "tree" model envisioned a unitary structure in which the EC's central institutions assumed authority for several policy "branches," including a justice and home affairs branch to be established *within* existing Community structures.

The Dutch draft treaty, which was not presented until the September 30, 1991, IGC meeting of foreign ministers, met with predictably fierce resistance by several member states. Denmark, the United Kingdom, and France refused to yield on their insistence that cooperation on justice and home affairs (pillar three), as well as foreign and security policy (pillar two), remain outside of the EC institutional framework. This opposition, combined with the fact that it was submitted late, helped to defeat the Dutch draft.

THE COMMISSION KEEPS TRYING: THE 1991 COMMUNICATIONS

Meanwhile—despite overtures to the Commission from the AHIG, which was working on a draft program on immigration and asylum matters to present at the December Maastricht Summit—the Commission proceeded to work independently on its own recommendations (de Jong 1995). The outlines of these recommendations were put forth in October 1991, in two Communications—one on the right of asylum (Commission 1991b) and another on immigration (Commission 1991c). Together, the two Communications promoted a "global approach" to immigration that emphasized "complementary, comprehensive, and realistic responses" (Commission 1991c:2, 19). The two documents outlined a strategy for extending harmonization beyond border initiatives and anticipated the possible extension of Community competence over additional immigration policy areas.

Emphasizing a spirit of accommodation, the Commission spoke of the need to move "beyond the legal debates as to which

53

authorities [the Commission or the Twelve] should be competent to take such measures" (Ibid.:13).[47] It limited its calls for harmonization to management and control areas, such as measures to combat illegal immigration[48] and, in its Communication on Asylum, to combating asylum "abuse." Among the initiatives recommended in the asylum area were the ratification of the Dublin Convention, the extension of a "parallel" convention to other countries, the streamlining of procedures for processing "manifestly unfounded" asylum claims, and the creation of standard criteria for receiving and processing asylum applications.

The Commission's proposals drew criticism from some immigrant advocates for their restrictive and exclusionary tone. However, one would be remiss to overlook the more forward-looking aspect of the October 1991 Communications. In designating three areas for "priority Community attention"—relieving migration pressures, controlling migration flows, and strengthening integration policies for legal immigrants—the Commission set forth the outlines of a strategy for a comprehensive Community immigration policy.[49] Despite its prior assertion that such sensitive issue areas as border controls and admission criteria should be settled through the intergovernmental process,[50] the Commission may have endorsed harmonization in certain "control" areas as a means of introducing, and eventually expanding, Community competence into immigration and asylum areas.

In retrospect, it is doubtful that the Commission could have pushed successfully for harmonization in any areas *other* than those having to do with regulation and control. A growing sense of vulnerability to political and economic developments in the former Soviet bloc, and a deepening economic recession in the West, added to the already heightened apprehension over asylum seekers and illegal immigrants. It is thus unlikely that member states

---

[47] It did so, however, while adding that its recommendations did not prejudge the results (i.e., competencies) proposed by the Intergovernmental Conference.

[48] The Communication on Immigration emphasized the importance of a "joint response . . . [in] improving control over immigration, without in any way prejudicing the right of asylum available to refugees who are genuine victims of persecution" (Commission 1991c:19).

[49] See the discussion on the February 1994 Commission Communication, pp. 83-85.

[50] See earlier discussion of the Commission Communication of December 7, 1988, pp. 29-30.

would have been receptive to Commission appeals for additional policy harmonization in the immigration area—an initiative that might have only served to isolate the Commission further.

THE DECEMBER 1991 WORK PROGRAM

Although the October 1991 Communications played no specific role in the subsequent report on harmonizing immigration and asylum policies submitted to the Maastricht Council by the Ministers Responsible for Immigration (see AHIG 1991c),[51] many of the themes and recommendations in those documents were echoed in the Ministers' report. For example, the Ministers identified five priority areas for continuing attention: admission policies; control of unauthorized immigration; labor migration policies; the situation of legally resident third-country nationals; and policies to address external migration pressures (Ibid:3-6).

With respect to admission policies, the Immigration Ministers called for establishing common family reunification policies as well as standard criteria for admitting individuals for employment, self-employment, and study. As for illegal immigration, the Ministers urged harmonization of efforts to prevent the employment of unauthorized individuals, the uniform application of expulsion principles, and cooperation with countries of emigration (or intermediary or transit countries) in order to stem clandestine immigration and prevent deported immigrants from re-entering Community space. On admission for the purpose of seeking asylum, the work program suggested that "unambiguous conditions" be established for determining "unjustified" claims, and called for the uniform definition and application of principles regarding the "first host country" and "countries [in which] there was generally no risk of persecution" (Ibid:8-9).

The Ministers went on to acknowledge that, in contrast to the free movement of EC nationals, "policy regarding third country nationals was still essentially the subject of national measures" (Ibid.:11). The work program thus recommended greater attention to the possibility of harmonizing employment and other rights of long-term legally resident TCNs. Finally, on the matter of migra-

---

[51] Both parts of the report—one concerning immigration and "alien rights" and the other asylum—included work programs and a timetable for their implementation.

tion pressures, the work program suggested that member states work to "define a common answer to the question of how . . . immigration pressure can be accommodated [in order] to make the problems manageable for the entire Community" (Ibid.:13).

The importance of these and other statements in the report cannot be over-emphasized. They are a formal acknowledgment by an intergovernmental body of high-level member-state officials that *strictly national policies* could not provide adequate responses to the Community-wide challenges of immigration and asylum. Policy harmonization was thus set up as a prerequisite to progress on these issues.

Not surprisingly, the Immigration Ministers perceived harmonization not "as an end in itself but as a means of re-orienting policies where such action makes for efficiency and speed of intervention" (Ibid.:3). In a long-overdue observation, they noted that harmonization on immigration and asylum matters had been elusive in large part because the ultimate implications of the Dublin and External Frontiers Conventions were "much greater than was perhaps originally expected" (Ibid.: 12).[52] Ratification of the two Conventions, they concluded, would serve as an indispensable "inducement to harmonize policy" (Ibid.:13).

The Ministers also acknowledged the importance of public perceptions for effective immigration policies:

> It is impossible to over-rate the importance which political circles must attach to the question of immigration policy in a period of great tension; the more the activities undertaken in the harmonization process are favorably perceived by society and the political world, the greater will be the chances of success (Ibid.:17).[53]

The Council adopted the Ministers' work program at the Maastricht Summit in December 1991. Despite progress in some areas, however, the Community remained a long way from imple-

---

[52] For example, assigning responsibility for the examination of asylum applications as specified in the Dublin Convention presupposes that member states have confidence in each other's asylum-determination systems. Harmonization of basic asylum policies thus becomes the next logical step toward giving this confidence some substance.

[53] This constituted one of the clearest acknowledgments yet of the correlation between (and importance of) popular perceptions and *collective* policy initiatives on immigration: success in the latter was now explicitly linked to quelling public concern about immigration.

menting both the broader goals of Article 8a (embodied in the concept of an internal frontier-free Europe) and many of the specific measures included in the Palma Document. The Coordinators acknowledged as much in their report to the Maastricht Council when they noted the continued disagreement over ". . . the interpretation and scope of the relevant Treaty provisions, *inter alia* Article 8a of the EEC Treaty, and the obligations flowing therefrom, the extent to which political decisions in this field had already been taken, and where the competence for taking decisions and action lay" (Coordinators' Group 1991c:2). The Coordinators urged the Maastricht Council to use its authority to impress upon member states the importance of reaching a "convergent interpretation" with the Commission on Article 8a. It also asked the Council to help resolve the dispute between Spain and the United Kingdom over Gibraltar—a dispute that continued to halt progress on the External Frontiers Convention.

4. MAASTRICHT AND THE TREATY ON EUROPEAN UNION

he Maastricht Summit of December 1991 was intended to launch the European Union. Having abandoned the Dutch draft treaty at the September IGC meeting, member states opted to structure the new European Union along the "pillar" design outlined in the Luxembourg plan.

The **Treaty on European Union** approved by the Maastricht Council thus distinguishes between matters that fall under the competence of the Community and those to be addressed principally through intergovernmental cooperation. The TEU establishes three policy "pillars." The first comprises the three former Communities (ECSC, EEC, and Euratom) and pertains to matters over which the Community has competence. The second and third pillars—both intergovernmental, with decision-making requiring unanimity—deal with matters relating, respectively, to Common Foreign and Security Policy and Justice and Home Affairs (JHA). Except for certain integration and citizenship matters, virtually all immigration and asylum matters fall under the Treaty's third, or JHA, pillar (Title VI).

THE THIRD PILLAR AND PROSPECTS FOR COMMUNITY COMPETENCE

espite its intergovernmental character, the third pillar anticipates more common strategy on immigration policy. Thus, within the third pillar, **Article K.1** of the TEU outlines nine areas to be regarded by member states as matters of *common interest* in achieving the objectives of the Union. The nine areas are:

(1) Asylum policy[54];
(2) Rules governing the crossing of the Community's external borders;
(3) Immigration policy and policy regarding TCNs;
(4) Combating drug addiction (insofar as this is not covered by items 7-9);
(5) Combating fraud on an international scale;
(6) Judicial cooperation in civil matters;
(7) Judicial cooperation in criminal matters;
(8) Customs cooperation; and
(9) Police cooperation for the purposes of preventing and combating terrorism, unlawful drug trafficking, and other serious forms of international crime.

Immigration was thus included as a law enforcement matter alongside criminal and police-related issues.

For advocates of greater Community competence on immigration issues, **Article K.3** may be more important. This Article grants the Commission the right of *co-initiative* on immigration matters and sets up an extensive "consultation and collaboration" procedure for Community decision-making.[55] In addition to granting the Commission the right to initiate policy, Article K.3 states

---

[54] The Treaty also includes a "Declaration on Asylum" in its Final Act: "[T]he Council will consider as a matter of priority questions concerning Member States' asylum policies, with the aim of adopting, by the beginning of 1993, common action to harmonize aspects of them, in the light of the work programme and timetable contained in the report on asylum drawn up at the request of the European Council meeting in Luxembourg on 28 and 29 June 1991. In this connection, the Council will also consider, by the end of 1993, on the basis of a report, the possibility of applying Article K.9 to such matters" (European Communities 1992:247).

[55]The Article also specifies the various decision-making mechanisms available to the Council: (1) joint positions, (2) joint actions, and (3) the elaboration of conventions. Specifically, Article K.3 states that "[t]he Council may, on the initiative of any member state *or of the Commission* in the areas referred to in Article K.1(1) to (6), or on the initiative of any Member State in the areas referred to Article K.1 (7) to (9), adopt *joint positions* and promote . . . cooperation contributing to the pursuit of the objectives of the Union; adopt *joint action* in so far as the objectives of the Union can be attained better by joint action than by the Member States acting individually; . . . [and] without prejudice to Article 220 of the Treaty, *draw up conventions* which it shall recommend to Member States for adoption. Unless otherwise provided by such conventions, measures implementing them shall be adopted within the Council by a majority of two-thirds of the High Contracting Parties. Such conventions may stipulate that the Court of Justice shall have jurisdiction to interpret their provisions and to rule on any disputes regarding their application" (European Communities 1992:133; emphases added). As noted in a December 10, 1993, Commission Communication, this last provision is significant in that it prevents member states from concluding conventions in the areas listed in Article K.1 "in the traditional manner prescribed by public international law" (Commission 1993c:6).

that the Council may elect to grant the European Court of Justice jurisdiction to interpret and arbitrate disputes arising from community policies (see European Communities 1992:132).

Article K.9 may be even more significant with respect to the Community's eventual competence on immigration and related matters. It describes the mechanism by which competence over the first six of Article K.1's common interest areas can be transfered from the intergovernmental to the Community pillar, thus creating an opening for greater Community authority in immigration matters.[56]

Although the TEU opted for intergovernmental cooperation on immigration matters by placing them under the third pillar, it also strengthened the authority of the Community's central institutions. By granting the Commission the right of co-initiative in areas previously reserved for member states, it linked the Commission more closely to work in the immigration and asylum areas. Similarly, the TEU granted the European Parliament consultation authority on proposed legislation while denying it the right of full scrutiny of Community policies, and it charged the ECJ with implementing and adjudicating disputes arising from such policies under specified conditions. Finally, the Treaty's procedural provisions for the possible transfer of certain issue areas to the Community's competence raised expectations that a comprehensive common strategy in these policy realms could be achieved.

DASHED HOPES, NATIONAL RETRENCHMENT

As has so often been the case, performance did not live up to promise. After pre-Summit hype and post-Summit euphoria subsided, Europe before and after Maastricht was virtually indistin-

---

[56] Article K.9 states that "the Council, acting *unanimously* on *the initiative of the Commission* or a Member State, may decide to apply Article 100c of the Treaty establishing the European Community to action areas referred to in Article K.1 (1) to (6), and at the same time determine the relevant voting conditions relating to it. It shall recommend the Member States to adopt that decision in accordance with their respective constitutional requirements" (European Communities 1992:135; emphasis added). Article 100c—which was added to the Treaty at the request of the Dutch Foreign Minister during the IGC deliberations—moves visa policy into the competence of the EC by requiring that the Council determine the third countries whose nationals must be in possession of a visa when crossing the external frontiers of the Community. Council decision-making on any of the (1) to (6) issue areas were to be made by unanimity until January 1, 1996; thereafter, by qualified majority. As opposed to Article K.3, which grants the Commission a *shared right of initiative* with member states, Article K.9 gives the Commission the *exclusive right* to initiate policy once it secures competence over an issue area (Ibid.:135; emphases added).

guishable with respect to immigration matters. In fact, one is hard-pressed to identify significant progress in either process or outcome on a broad array of long-standing issues as member states again favored national solutions to what are increasingly perceived to be *national* challenges.

Although the Maastricht Summit was hailed at the time as a watershed event in the movement toward more complete European integration, the Treaty's subsequent ratification "woes"—its initial rejection by the Danes and narrow passage by the French—quickly suggested that the European public was far more ambivalent about the direction taken by Brussels than had previously been assumed.

In addition, the post-Maastricht lull may be attributed in part to the onset of economic and social self-doubt and renewed nationalism among key European actors. These were caused by the enormous costs of assisting the former Soviet bloc countries in their transition to democratic capitalism, the asylum (and feared mass-migration) implications of the crises in the Balkans and the former Soviet Union, a deepening and widening economic recession, and growing public antagonism toward resident foreigners.

For example, a now-united Germany, long a chief advocate of harmonized Community immigration and asylum policies, slowly came to the conclusion that it could no longer look to the EU to solve its immediate asylum problems. A divisive debate over the country's constitutional guarantee of asylum grew more audible. In mid-1993, it led to the amendment of Germany's constitution (see Papademetriou with Kamali Miyamoto 1996).[57] The center-right coalition in France also rode to an extraordinary electoral triumph on a wave of anti-foreigner public opinion. The rise of such sentiments throughout Western Europe provided politicians of the right with ample "capital" as they adopted restrictive national responses to immigration in country after country.

Whether Maastricht represented a new peak in the evolution of Europe has been the subject of a clamorous debate. Even those who look sympathetically at what they view as a largely inexorable march toward a more collective European identity were perplexed by Maastricht's rather meager payoffs. The most compelling explanation for the slow pace of progress may lie in the reluctance, and

---

[57] Some modifications of the constitution would have been necessary in any event, to facilitate Germany's implementation of the Schengen Agreement and its participation in the Dublin Convention.

in some cases outright refusal, of more and more member states—and growing proportions of their populations—to surrender their sovereign prerogatives on an increasing number of social, cultural, and political issues. Alternatively, the slow pace of evolution may simply be a natural by-product of the unanticipated break in momentum generated by the Treaty's ratification difficulties and Europe's understandable preoccupation with the fundamental organizational dilemmas these difficulties brought to the surface.

The Commission—so often the Community's intellectual, political, and administrative motivator on such matters—and key member states experienced pronounced bureaucratic inertia on the immigration and asylum fronts as they became preoccupied with politically more pressing issues, such as the quagmire in former Yugoslavia, the deepening economic downturn (particularly unemployment, which averaged about 12 percent in the Community in 1993), world trade negotiations, and their own electoral upheavals. Final closure on the two conventions that had preoccupied Europe most during the Single European Act period—the Dublin and External Frontiers Conventions—remained elusive.[58]

PUSH AHEAD OR PULL BACK?

Events in 1992 sapped Europe's energy for deeper integration and added to the dissonance regarding the merits of a more "federal" Europe. Popular antagonism toward the Brussels' bureaucracy—perceived as intrusive, aloof, high-handed, and politically unaccountable—spread rapidly in most Western European countries[59] and strengthened the hands of those who

---

[58] Once ratified, the conventions would face the arduous task of implementation in a not-yet-fully-defined "federal" setting. Article 26 of the External Frontiers Convention, for instance, requires the establishment of a committee "comprising one representative of the Government of each member state and chaired by the Member State holding the Council Presidency, to examine general questions concerning application or interpretation of this Convention . . . [and to] unanimously take [the] decisions necessary for [its] proper application. The Committee may, however, acting unanimously, draw up a list of cases in which it shall take decisions by a majority of two-thirds. At the request of a Member State representative, the Committee may defer its decision for up to two months after establishing a common position on a proposal put to the Committee. The Committee shall determine its own rules of procedure and can set up working parties in preparation for taking a decision" (see AHIG 1991b:28).

[59] The direction of this line of argument is ironic and counterintuitive for two reasons. First, one of the most effective ways to ensure greater accountability and transparency in Community decision-making is clearly through further integration, in which the European Parliament and Court of Justice would be given greater authority to probe Community

opposed further integration, since it would have meant further empowering the Commission's widely disliked mandarins. The chorus was led by the United Kingdom, although—depending on the issue—Denmark and a less conspicuous group of smaller southern European countries often joined in. The resentment was stoked from all sides of the political spectrum—by those who opposed the sovereignty-eroding effects of a stronger Union as well as those who were eager to blame Brussels for a vast array of real and imagined "misdeeds."

CONTINUING CONTROVERSY OVER ARTICLE 8A

Apparently tone-deaf to the changing political landscape, the Commission renewed its efforts to break the logjam on the issue of free movement of persons within a frontier-free space. It did so by seeking to "clarify" the scope and implications of Article 8a (Article 7a in the TEU). Most analysts interpret Article 8a as applying not only to the persons explicitly referred to in the Rome Treaty's Articles 48 to 66 (economically active nationals *of member states*) but also to legally resident nationals of non-member countries. As Vos (1992) observes, although member states in the post-Maastricht era regard immigration as an area of common interest, the conclusion that Article 8a implies a frontier-free area for *all* persons "cannot be in dispute." The logic is compelling. Freedom of movement necessarily implies complete abolition of controls on all individuals who cross internal borders, irrespective of their nationality. Any other interpretation would render Article 8a irrelevant. Nevertheless, the United Kingdom, Ireland, and Denmark insist that limited documentation checks on persons entering these countries from another member state *are compatible* with Article 8a (see also, Collinson 1994:45).

On May 8, 1992, in a Communication to the Council and the Parliament entitled "Abolition of Border Controls," the Commission assessed progress on the removal of controls on intra-Community movement of goods, services, capital, *and people.* It noted

---

decisions. Second, the Community's reputation for a "culture of secrecy" stemmed first and foremost from the methods and procedures employed in the Community's *intergovernmental* deliberations. Compared to these activities, the Commission's own deliberations appear *almost* "democratic'—or at least as democratic as complex, rigid, and high-handed international bureaucracies can be expected to be.

that, while the goals of free movement of goods, services, and capital were well on their way to realization, the free movement of people remained mired in competing legal interpretations. For its part, the Commission had no doubt. It insisted that:

> [The] phrase 'free movement of . . . persons' in Article 8a refers to all persons, whether or not they are economically active and irrespective of their nationality. The internal market could not operate under conditions equivalent to those in a national market if the movement of individuals within this market were hindered by controls at internal frontiers (Commission 1992b:10).

The Commission also noted that "the situation is worrying at all political levels where freedom of movement of individuals is concerned . . . Lack of political consensus on the actual scope of Article 8a is still apparent" (Ibid.:1).

RESTRICTING ACCESS TO ASYLUM

With the Article 8a matter still unsettled, member states proceeded with uncharacteristic determination to discuss asylum, one of Europe's gravest policy and political challenges, and one of the issues on which progress toward an internal frontier-free Europe hinged. The focus of that effort was the Dublin Convention—the Community's principal vehicle for harmonizing asylum policy—which had been revised and refined in an unsuccessful effort to bring reluctant member states on board.

Some member states were concerned that acceding to the Convention would imply *de facto* endorsement of another state's legal and regulatory asylum-adjudication mechanisms, and thus the possible dilution of national humanitarian and protection standards. Moreover, some states had already ratified various international refugee-protection and human-rights accords and were concerned that a blanket acceptance of the Convention's criteria would raise fundamental constitutional and legal issues for them.

Although ratification of the Dublin Convention continued to languish, a number of practical asylum-related issues received further vetting. The Ad Hoc Immigration Group's Subgroup on Asylum began to examine the possibility of developing a computerized fingerprint identification system (EURODAC) to deter multiple filings by asylum seekers. Similarly, AHIG began to look into creating a clearinghouse on asylum (CIREA) in the Council Secretariat to facilitate information exchange on such issues as developments in principal sending countries (see box **4-1**, p.68 for more detailed descriptions of EURODAC and CIREA.)

In keeping with the Maastricht program on asylum, Immigration Ministers increased their efforts to limit *male fide* applicants' access to asylum. This issue was politically important in a number of European countries, particularly Germany, where asylum applications nearly doubled between 1991 and 1992 and were fueling an increasingly ugly domestic debate (see table **4-2**, pp. 70-71). Meeting in London on November 30, 1992, the Ministers approved two resolutions and a series of conclusions in an attempt to address the issue of fraudulent claims.

The **Resolution on manifestly unfounded applications for asylum** recommended that accelerated processing procedures be employed in cases where there was "clearly no substance to an applicant's claim to fear persecution" or where "the claim is based on deliberate deception or is an abuse of the asylum procedure" (AHIG 1993a [Part II.C]:2). Applications lacking "substance" included those filed by individuals seeking employment or a better life or by applicants who could have found "readily available" protection somewhere in their own country. "Deliberate deception" involved the use of fraudulent documents and/or identification.

The **Resolution on a harmonized approach to questions concerning host third countries** provided for the immediate removal of asylum claimants who had passed through a "host third country" (i.e., a country in which they could have, or already had, received protection).

Finally, a set of **Conclusions on countries in which there is generally no serious risk of persecution** suggested that asylum applicants from designated "safe" countries be automatically returned to their country of origin if they were unable to provide evidence rebutting the assumption that their country did not generate refugees (see AHIG 1993a [Part II.B]:1-4).[60] It further recom-

---

[60] Both the Resolution on manifestly unfounded applications and this Conclusion were based on an AHIG report which identified a number of "safe countries," or "countries in which there is generally no serious risk of persecution." That report placed a strong emphasis on the creation of a reliable information exchange system on which assessments could be based (including such factors as a country's previous refugee admissions and recognition rates, its observance of human rights, the existence of democratic institutions, and political stability), and had noted the importance of relying on as wide a range of information sources as possible, including information from the UNHCR. It also precluded an applicant's "summary exclusion," although member states would be allowed to utilize the

mended that a country use the accelerated procedures reserved for manifestly unfounded asylum applications if an asylum applicant had passed through a "safe" country outside the EC and could be returned (AHIG 1993a [Part II.D]:1-5). This fast-track method also provided for a streamlined appeal process, requiring that an initial decision on such cases be reached within one month. The Group called for incorporating these principles into national law by January 1, 1995.

The Edinburgh Council adopted these resolutions and conclusions[61] at its December 1992 meeting. This action raised a chorus of well-founded concerns among refugee advocates and some analysts who feared that access to the asylum systems of many EC member states would become severely restricted—as indeed it has been. The Immigration Ministers' subsequent adoption at their June 1993 meeting in Copenhagen of such non-binding Resolutions as those on **"harmonization of national policies on family reunification"**[62] and the setting of **"guidelines [on] admission of particularly vulnerable persons from the former Yugoslavia"**[63] did little to allay fears of an evolving "Fortress Europe" mentality.

---

accelerated procedures for rejecting "manifestly unfounded" claimants. Finally, the report made recommendations pertaining to people displaced by the conflict in Yugoslavia, practices to be followed by member states on expulsion, and transit for the purpose of expulsion (see Council 1992b [Annex II]).

[61] The Edinburgh Council also approved a declaration recognizing "the danger" and the "destabilizing" effects of uncontrolled immigration, and stressed the importance of "analyzing the causes of immigration pressure, and ... ways of removing [them]" (European Council 1992:54). Like a similar observation by the Commission in October of 1991, this was a precursor to the later articulation of a "root causes" approach to migration (discussed below).

[62] This Resolution, which applies to relatives of long-term legally resident TCNs, attempts to establish uniform definitions of "family," while allowing member states to specify admission criteria. The European Parliament criticized the Resolution in July 1993, for its likely failure to protect the privacy of relevant individuals (see Bunyan and Webber 1995:17-18 and Collinson 1994:45).

[63] The six largest recipients of displaced persons from Yugoslavia (Germany, Austria, Denmark, Norway, Sweden, and Switzerland) spearheaded efforts to share the costs of admitting displaced persons from the region. Having failed to reach any kind of "burden-sharing" agreement (a misguided term in the view of many refugee advocates for its emphasis on "burdens," rather than legal and moral responsibilities), Immigration Ministers sought instead to establish a common approach allowing for the temporary protection for victims of civil war. The Resolution noted, however, that "wherever possible," assistance should be provided to such individuals "in the region of origin . . . in safe areas situated as close as possible to their homes" (AHIG 1993b:3). Close-to-final resolution on this matter would not occur until June 1995, after failed efforts to reach agreement in November 1993, January 1994 (in the Vienna Group), and December 1994. At the June 21, 1995 meeting of the JHA Council, representatives of all 15 EU member states agreed to the text of a resolution on sharing the costs of temporary protection for individuals displaced by civil war (see *Migration News Sheet* 1995g:5).

4-1. EU FORA FOR EXCHANGING INFORMATION

A pilot study for the *European Automated Fingerprinting Recognition System (EURODAC)* was approved by the AHIG in June 1993. Like the Schengen Information System (see box **3-1**, pp. 26-27), the EURODAC connects national fingerprint databases (containing the prints of all asylum applicants) with a central database. Since the creation of such a system is not authorized by the Dublin Convention, the AHIG worked to establish a separate agreement for its creation. It has been suggested that, while the technical feasibility of such a network is studied, fingerprints could be exchanged between states on a bilateral basis.

The Immigration Ministers lent support to the establishment of the *Center for Information, Discussion and Exchange on Asylum (CIREA)* at their November 1992 meeting in London. CIREA is intended to facilitate information exchange on such asylum-related matters as the sources of migration pressure in sending countries, information on transit countries, and the various asylum procedures and policies of EC member states. It is run by the Council Secretariat.

On December 1, 1992, the Immigration Ministers approved the establishment of the *Center for Information, Discussion, and Exchange on the Crossing of Borders and Immigration (CIREFI)* to assist in the implementation of the External Frontiers Convention, including the examination of individual member-state laws regarding carrier sanctions. In November 1994, the K.4 Committee (see box **5-1**, p. 76) recommended that CIREFI be progressively strengthened to assist member states in preventing unauthorized immigration and illegal residence, combating immigration crime, detecting forged documents, and improving expulsion procedures, beginning on January 1, 1995. Since that date, a permanent monthly conference has been convened within CIREFI to address these matters. CIREFI is not authorized to give instructions to member-state authorities, nor is it intended to effect closer cooperation among member states.

Sources: Cruz 1993, AHIG 1993c, AHIG 1993d, Commission 1992e, and JHA Council 1994d.

As the end of 1993 approached, the Ad Hoc Immigration Group prepared its "Report on the completion of the Maastricht program on asylum adopted in 1991." In it, the AHIG Subgroup on Asylum outlined its intent to focus on the numerous technical, administrative, and policy issues on which ratification of the Dublin Convention depended. Among these were the following: interpretation of the Convention's articles; reception and transfer arrangements for asylum seekers; development of a standard form and timetables for determining the member state responsible for examining an asylum claim; an inventory of residence permits; the establishment of CIREA; measures to combat asylum fraud; harmonization of substantive legal rules on asylum and expulsion; and closure on a list of "safe countries" (see AHIG 1993f).[64] The pace and intensity of work on asylum led the Immigration Ministers to predict that the Dublin Convention would probably come into force in the first half of 1994—a characteristic overstatement.

COMBATING ILLEGAL IMMIGRATION

The Immigration Ministers also stepped up their efforts to establish a common approach to the problem of illegal immigration. At their meeting on November 30-December 1, 1992, they approved the establishment of the **Center for Information, Discussion, and Exchange on the Crossing of Borders and Immigration (CIREFI)** to assist in the examination of member-state laws regarding carrier sanctions and other measures for implementing the External Frontiers Convention (see box **4-1**, p. 68). Not long thereafter, AHIG presented a **Draft Recommendation concerning checks on and expulsion of third-country nationals residing or working without authorization** to the Immigration Ministers meeting in Copenhagen in June 1993. The draft outlined the conditions under which

---

[64] The report noted the progress made toward drafting joint assessments of the situations in sending countries (reports on Albania and Angola were expected shortly, to be followed by assessments of Bulgaria, China, Iraq, Vietnam, Zaire, Turkey, and Nigeria). It also pointed to progress on preliminary contacts with Norway, Sweden, Finland, Switzerland, Austria, Poland, the Czech Republic, Slovakia, and Canada on a Convention to parallel the Dublin Convention, noting, however, that these negotiations hinged on ratification of the Dublin Convention. Finally, the report indicated that member states were "in principle willing to admit certain groups of persons [e.g., persons displaced from the former Yugoslavia] temporarily . . . in accordance with national possibilities and in the context of a coordinated action by all Member States" (AHIG 1993f:19).

4-2. Asylum Applications in Selected Western European Countries,[a] in thousands, with percentages accepted in parentheses

	1980	1985	1990	1991
Austria	9.3	6.7	22.8	27.3
		(14.5)	(7.0)	(12.0)
Belgium	2.7	5.3	13.0	15.4
				(1.6)
France	18.8	28.8	54.8	47.4
		(40.0)	(15.7)	(19.7)
Germany	107.8	73.8	193.1	256.1
	(12.0)	(29.2)	(4.4)	(6.9)
Italy	1.5	5.4	4.7	31.7
	(28.6)		(28.0)	(4.7)
The Netherlands	1.3	5.6	21.2	21.6
		(17.4)	(6.6)	(6.3)
Sweden	5.6[c]	14.5	29.4	27.4
			(85.0)	(80.0)
Switzerland	6.1	9.7	35.8	41.6
	(41.9)	(10.0)	(4.9)	(3.0)
United Kingdom	n.a.	4.4	26.2	44.8
		(13.0)	(3.5)	(1.3)

[a] Data do not accurately reflect how many asylum seekers are still in the country. Annual totals can also include persons who have been counted more than once, or who have already left the country. They also may include persons who only stayed a week or so in transit to a third country, as well as persons who left after a few days. Interpretation of the data is further complicated by the fact that some countries include in their tallies the number of principal asylum applicants and their dependents, while others include only the number of principal applicants; for instance, data for Austria and the U.K. refer to principal applicants only, while data for Germany include principal applicants and their dependents.

[b] Asylum approved rate is for the first 6 months.

[c] This is an approximate figure for individuals granted asylum (including dependents). According to the Swedish Ministry of Labor, in 1980 the total number of persons claiming asylum was not much higher than that of persons granted asylum.

4-2, continued

1992	1993	1994	1995	
16.2	4.7	5.1	5.9	Austria
(9.8)	(7.8)	(7.4)	(12.5)	
17.3	26.3	14.3	11.4	Belgium
(1.5)	(1.1)	(1.5)	n.a.	
28.9	27.6	26.0	20.6	France
(29.1)	(28.0)	(20.0)	(11.6)	
438.2	322.8	127.2	127.9	Germany
(4.3)	(3.2)	(7.3)	(9.0)	
2.6	1.6	1.8	1.7[b]	Italy
(9.8)	(8.4)	(16.9)	(15.0)	
20.3	35.4	52.6	29.3	The Netherlands
(32.6)	(23.0)	(37.6)	(36.4)	
84.0	37.6	18.6	9.0	Sweden
(65.0)	(97.0)		(27.0)	
18.0	24.7	16.1	17.0	Switzerland
(4.5)	(13.6)	(12.5)	(16.4)	
24.6	22.4	32.8	44.0	United Kingdom
(4.5)	(7.1)	(4.0)	(5.0)	

Sources: *Trends in International Migration* (Paris: Organisation for Economic Co-operation and Development) [OECD]), 1995; Secretariat of the Inter-Governmental Consultations on Asylum, Refugees and Migration Policies in Europe, North America and Australia; *World Refugee Survey 1996* (Washington, D.C.: U.S. Committee for Refugees).

4-3. EUROPOL

The idea of a *European Police Office (Europol)* received official backing during the Luxembourg European Council on June 28-29, 1991, when German Chancellor Kohl proposed the creation of a European Criminal Police Office to combat international and European crime, especially drug trafficking. The Kohl proposal resulted in the establishment of the Ad Hoc Working Group on Europol in August 1991 and in preparatory meetings organized by the United Kingdom in 1991 and 1992. Work on the Convention establishing Europol began under the Belgian Council Presidency, although the thorny issue of the role of the European Court of Justice was put aside at these preliminary meetings.

Because of Europol's drug-related responsibilities, its development is under the responsibility of the Trevi Group Ministers. Considered a coordinating rather than an investigative body for its first few years of operation, Europol is intended to monitor the activities of such bodies as national police, international police (Interpol), and CELAD (see box **3-3**, p. 32).

The Treaty on European Union refers to "the organization of a Union-wide system of exchanging information within a Europol. " At its October 29, 1993, meeting, the Council set a deadline of October 1994 for completion of the Convention on Europol, while noting the progress on the establishment of the EDU, Europol's predecessor. The EDU became operational in The Hague on February 16, 1994, and has helped to expedite information exchanges between member-state police forces and customs authorities with respect to illegal drug trafficking, money laundering, and criminal investigations.

The Europol Convention received "priority" attention under the Greek, German, and French Presidencies. The German Presidency, in particular, put tremendous effort into preparation of the Convention text. At the December 1994 Essen Summit, Germany, Italy, and the Benelux countries urged that the Europol Convention be concluded by the June 1995 Cannes Summit. The Council also recommended that the EDU's mandate be expanded to include, *inter alia*, the fight against the "smuggling of persons." At an informal meeting in January 1995, France agreed to comply with Spain's insistence that Europol's mandate be extended to cover terrorism. However, France called for a two-year period after the signing of the Convention during which signatories would arrive at a satisfactory definition of a terrorist.

A meeting of the EU Interior Ministers in Brussels on March 10, 1995, removed many obstacles to creating Europol, clearing the Convention for likely signature at the Cannes Summit. Although France promised that Europol would be a central facet of its EU presidency, member states deadlocked in Cannes over who should be authorized to arbitrate conflicts. Germany and the Benelux countries sought to use the Convention to introduce Community competence into third-pillar issue areas by granting the Court of Justice final jurisdiction in disputes stemming from the agency's operation. The United Kingdom, with the support of some Scandinavian countries, objected to this provision, arguing that criminal law is an important preserve of national governments. The Netherlands refused to concede to British demands, insisting that EU citizens must have some ability to defend their rights before an independent Court. In the end, member states agreed to sign the Europol Convention, but to delay the decision over which courts shall interpret its application until June 1996. The Convention must be ratified by all 15 member states before it can come into force. The Benelux countries have vowed that they will not ratify it until a satisfactory solution is found to the arbitration issue. Germany, Italy, and Austria have also urged resolution of the dispute. Until the Convention is finalized, Europol (based in The Hague) will have a narrow mandate that focuses mainly on stolen cars and trafficking of drugs, people, and nuclear materials.

Sources: European Communities 1992, European Council 1994b, Hix 1995, and *Financial Times* 1995a.

unauthorized workers and residents in the Community should be expelled. It recommended that CIREFI be charged with facilitating information exchanges in order to help identify such individuals (AHIG 1993d:6).

The Ministers also agreed in Copenhagen to create a **European Drugs Unit (EDU)**, to begin its activities in The Hague the following January. The EDU was intended to speed up information exchanges between member-state police and customs forces as part of a common effort to combat drug trafficking and money laundering, paving the way for the eventual transition to **Europol**, the European Police Office (see box **4-3**, p. 72).

THE COMMISSION EXERCISES RESTRAINT

Progress on other immigration issues continued to be meager, however. Disputes over the intent of Article 8a and the issue of Community competence remained essentially unresolved. Furthermore, the year or so prior to the TEU's entry into force saw a retreat by the Commission—initially perhaps unintended, but gradually more conscious—from its usual role as sponsor of bold new initiatives. Many of its earlier proposals had been interpreted as thinly veiled attempts to capture primacy in areas where it had no direct competence. Now the Commission appeared to be concentrating primarily on offering support and "expert" assistance to the intergovernmental process.

5. IMMIGRATION, REFUGEE, AND ASYLUM ISSUES UNDER THE EUROPEAN UNION

T he formal launching of the **European Union** on November 1, 1993, led to the emergence of new Treaty-dictated structures and a not-insignificant redistribution of power. These changes spawned substantial and probably inevitable bureaucratic confusion, especially on the relationship between the areas on which the Union has competence (first pillar) and the areas on which competence is intergovernmental (second and third pillars). In the Union's early months, this confusion was compounded by an inattentive, inconsistent, and controversial Greek Presidency[65] and by the effort necessary to complete negotiations for enlarging the Union.

THE K.4 COMMITTEE AND INTERGOVERNMENTAL COORDINATION

O ne of the TEU's more significant organizational changes with respect to immigration matters was the creation of the **K.4 Committee**, named for Article K.4 (Title VI) (see box **5-1**, p. 76). The K.4 Committee was designed in part (a) to address duplication and organizational competition among the plethora of *ad hoc*

---

[65] Greek elections in the fall of 1993 had returned an ailing Andreas Papandreou as Prime Minister after a four-year absence. In addition, a bitter EU-Greek disagreement over "Macedonia," which included a formal EU challenge to Greece's embargo against the Republic of Macedonia in the European Court, interfered with good working relationships among EU member states. Greek relations were particularly tense with Germany, which Greece blamed directly and publicly for the quagmire in the former Yugoslavia. The inability of Greece to bring timely closure to the enlargement negotiations (and the brusque stepping in and taking over of the negotiations by Germany), followed by the failure of the Corfu Council to agree on a successor to Commission President Delors, contributed further to the impression of a "failed" Greek Presidency.

5-1. THE K.4 COMMITTEE

Article K.4 (Title VI) of the Treaty on European Union, entitled "Provisions on Cooperation in the Fields of Justice and Home Affairs," sets up a Coordinating Committee of senior officials to advise the Council. Like the Coordinators' Group it replaces, the K.4 Committee is designed to coordinate the numerous *ad hoc* bodies and processes in the immigration area, but unlike the Coordinators' Group, it also has "political" authority over them. The K.4 Committee is charged not only with overall coordination but full responsibility over the various Justice/Interior dossiers dealing with Article K.1's areas of common interest. Priority areas include: (1) immigration and asylum; (2) security and law enforcement, including police and customs operations; and (3) judicial cooperation. The Committee is composed of one senior representative per member state, including one representative from the Commission. To fulfill its mandate, the Committee can impanel any working parties needed to implement these programs, endorse their terms of reference, and approve their work programs and timetables.

The need for such a body was recognized in the 1992 Coordinators' report to the Council that proposed creation of a "steering group" to identify problems, negotiate solutions, and facilitate prompt information exchanges, as a means of giving substance to the extensive "consultation and collaboration" requirements provided for in Article K.3. Further evidence of the K.4 Committee's importance can be gleaned from the way various countries jockeyed to shape how Article K.4 is interpreted. For instance, Germany reacted to the 1992 Coordinators' report on the Committee by noting that the report:

". . . [did] not affect the principle that each Member State is free to decide on the designation of its representative and the composition of its delegation. The Federal Republic of Germany will designate the German member of the Article K.4 Committee separately for each item on the agenda. In so doing, it will designate in each case an official from the Ministry responsible for the field in question according to the distribution of duties obtaining within the German Federal Government. Officials not designated as members for a particular time on the agenda may nonetheless state positions insofar as the sphere of responsibility of the Ministry which they represent is affected (Coordinators' Group 1992b:2)."

Italy, intensely interested at the time in furthering harmonization on these issues, noted that it construed the "ultimate authority" references in the report to pertain to ". . . all of the tasks of co-ordination, consultation, and preparation for the Council's discussions, as assigned by the Treaty to the [senior officials] making up the Committee, without any hierarchical implications." Italy also noted that it understood the "right of initiative" conferred on the Committee to refer to the "opinions given for the Council" (Ibid.:1)

Source: European Communities 1992, and Coordinators' Group 1992a and 1992b.

bodies touching on immigration matters prior to the coming into force of the European Union, as well as (b) to create an administrative structure where none had existed before. (Figures **5-2** and **5-3**, pp. 78-79, show the migration-related organizational structure of the European Community and the European Union, respectively, pre- and post-November 1993.) The K.4 Committee resulted from the recognition that obtaining closure on critical immigration issues required not only a much higher level of coordination within and cooperation among the relevant member-state ministries,[66] *but also a better-managed intergovernmental process.*

The K.4 Committee replaces the Coordinators' Group and superimposes a "political" authority over other bodies and processes.[67] The Committee submits its proposals and recommendations directly to the Committee of Permanent Representatives (COREPER), which in turn reports to the Justice and Home Affairs (JHA) Council.[68] The Committee has the ability not only to propose solutions but also to intervene, where necessary, to resolve differences on immigration matters.

The Committee's sweeping mandate initially suggested that it was a body to watch. The clear intent behind its creation was to

---

[66] This is a poorly appreciated issue that has enormous implications for a state's ability to attain its policy goals on the immigration/asylum issue. A big part of the challenge rests with the cross-cutting character of the matter, which leads to interdepartmental competition among agencies whose mandates and principal constituencies differ (see Papademetriou and Hamilton 1995 for a full discussion of this problem and its effect on coherence in both formulating and executing policy in advanced industrial societies.)

[67] In a far-reaching 1992 report to the Council (Coordinators' Group 1992a), the Coordinators' Group detailed its views on how the K.4 Committee might be organized, the challenges it would face, and the opportunities that its existence would likely create. The Coordinators anticipated that the Committee would initially build on the work already in progress—namely, the asylum and immigration work programs approved by the Maastricht Council, the plan to combat drugs adopted by the Rome Council, the action program embraced by the Trevi ministers in Dublin, and the Palma Document approved by the Madrid Council. The Committee's priority agenda, they estimated, would be anchored in three substantive issue areas, or "sectors": (a) immigration and asylum; (b) security and law enforcement, including police and customs operations; and (c) judicial cooperation (Ibid:4). Subsequent reports by the Coordinators on the structure of the K.4 Committee and its subsidiary bodies included a November 1992 report, entitled "Work Structures for Title VI [Justice and Home Affairs] of the Treaty on European Union." This report noted that, in June 1992, the Coordinators had asked the various bodies under their mandate—the Ad Hoc Group, the Trevi Group, CELAD, the Customs Mutual Assistance Group, and the Working Group on Judicial Cooperation—to submit broad outlines of the work they intended to carry out in 1993. These work outlines were to be transferred to the K.4 Committee (see Coordinators' Group 1992e:8-17).

[68] The JHA Council (sometimes referred to as the "JAI Council," after its French acronym) is comprised of ministers responsible for Title VI (third-pillar) issue areas.

5-2. Pre–November 1993 Organization of the Migration-Related Bodies of the European Community

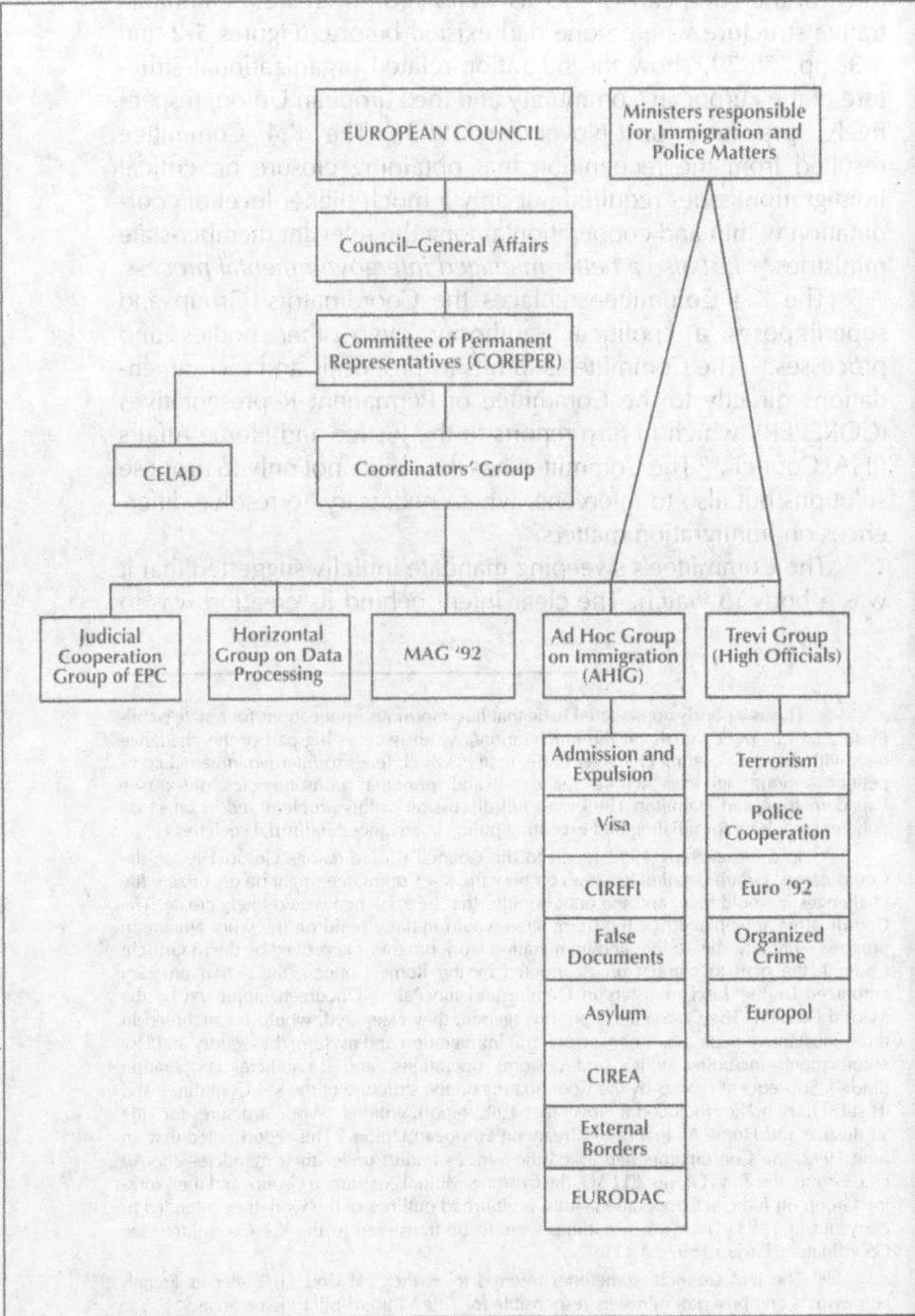

```
                    ┌─────────────────────┐   ┌─────────────────────┐
                    │  EUROPEAN COUNCIL   │   │ Ministers responsible│
                    └─────────────────────┘   │ for Immigration and │
                              │               │   Police Matters    │
                    ┌─────────────────────┐   └─────────────────────┘
                    │ Council–General Affairs │
                    └─────────────────────┘
                              │
                    ┌─────────────────────┐
                    │ Committee of Permanent │
                    │ Representatives (COREPER) │
                    └─────────────────────┘
                              │
    ┌────────┐      ┌─────────────────────┐
    │ CELAD  │──────│ Coordinators' Group │
    └────────┘      └─────────────────────┘
```

Judicial Cooperation Group of EPC	Horizontal Group on Data Processing	MAG '92	Ad Hoc Group on Immigration (AHIG)	Trevi Group (High Officials)
			Admission and Expulsion	Terrorism
			Visa	Police Cooperation
			CIREFI	Euro '92
			False Documents	Organized Crime
			Asylum	Europol
			CIREA	
			External Borders	
			EURODAC	

78

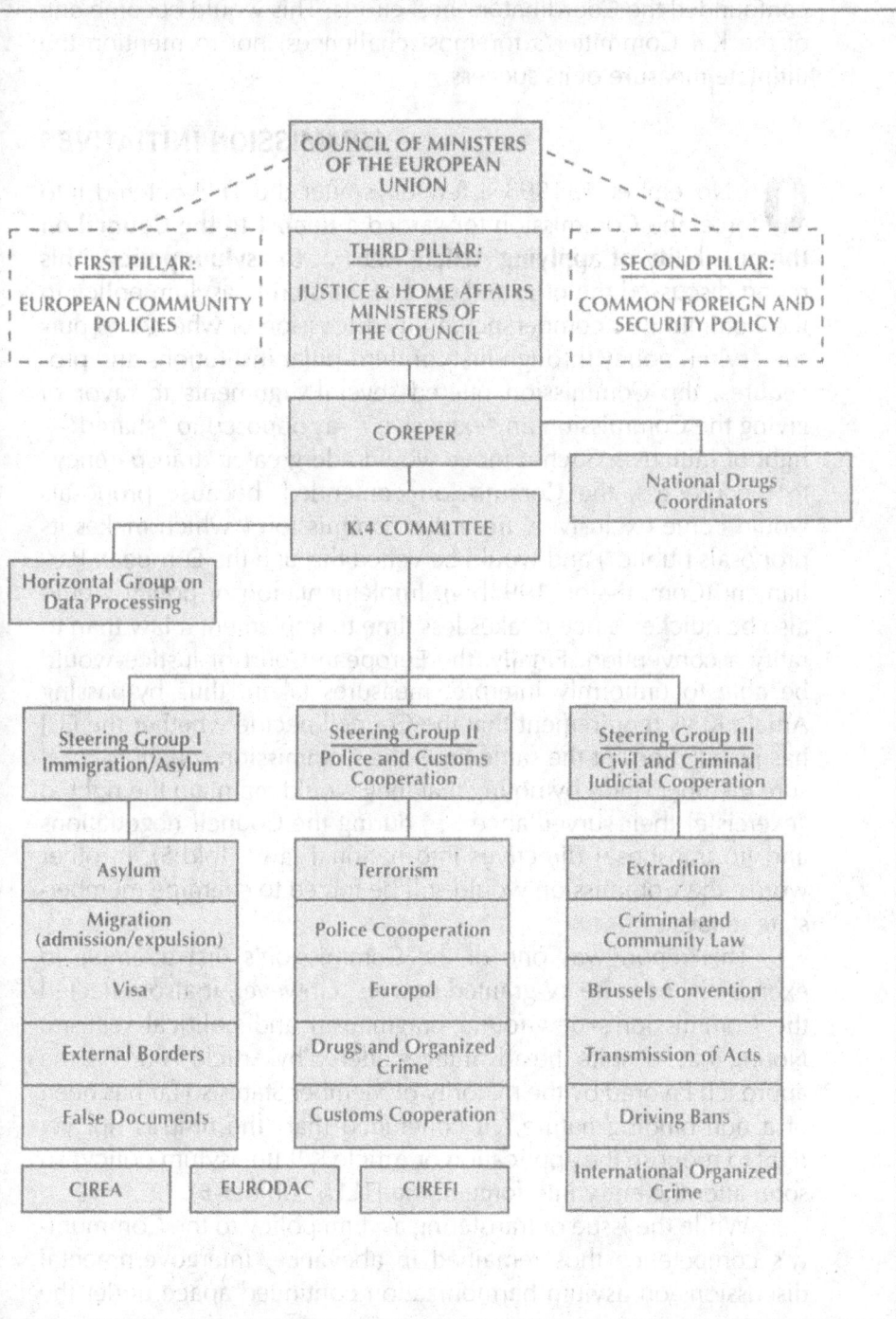

```
                    COUNCIL OF MINISTERS
                      OF THE EUROPEAN
                           UNION

FIRST PILLAR:          THIRD PILLAR:              SECOND PILLAR:
EUROPEAN COMMUNITY   JUSTICE & HOME AFFAIRS    COMMON FOREIGN AND
    POLICIES             MINISTERS OF            SECURITY POLICY
                         THE COUNCIL

                          COREPER

                                                  National Drugs
                                                  Coordinators

                        K.4 COMMITTEE

Horizontal Group on
  Data Processing


   Steering Group I        Steering Group II        Steering Group III
  Immigration/Asylum      Police and Customs         Civil and Criminal
                             Cooperation           Judicial Cooperation


       Asylum                  Terrorism                Extradition

      Migration                                        Criminal and
 (admission/expulsion)     Police Coooperation        Community Law

        Visa                   Europol              Brussels Convention

   External Borders       Drugs and Organized      Transmission of Acts
                                Crime

   False Documents        Customs Cooperation          Driving Bans

                                                   International Organized
     CIREA      EURODAC         CIREFI                    Crime
```

enable the Council to take decisions on issues that had thus far confounded the Coordinators' best efforts. This would become one of the K.4 Committee's foremost challenges, not to mention the ultimate measure of its success.

COMMISSION INITIATIVES

On November 4, 1993 a few days after the TEU entered into force, the Commission forwarded a **Report to the Council on the possibility of applying Article K.9 . . . to asylum policy**. This report discussed the pros and cons of transferring asylum policy to the Community's competence. In its discussion of whether to pursue asylum policy through first- or third-pillar institutions and procedures, the Commission offered several arguments in favor of giving the Commission an "exclusive"—as opposed to "shared"— right of initiative. Such a move would add greater "transparency" to the process, the Commission contended, because proposals would come exclusively from the Commission ("which makes its proposals public") and would be vetted through the European Parliament (Commission 1993b:4). Implementation of policy would also be quicker, since it takes less time to implement a law than to ratify a convention. Finally, the European Court of Justice would be able to uniformly interpret measures taken, thus by-passing Article K.3's requirement that the Council decide whether the ECJ has jurisdiction. At the same time, the Commission sought to reassure member states by noting that they would maintain the right to "exercis[e] their surveillance . . . during the Council negotiations and [to transpose] directives into national law" (Ibid:5). In other words, the Commission would still be forced to examine member-state requests.

This report was one of the Commission's first attempts to exercise its new Treaty-granted powers. However, it also reflected the Commission's new-found pragmatism and political realism. Noting that "despite the advantages offered by Article 100c . . . the approach favored by the majority of Member States so far has been of a non-binding nature," it concluded that "the time is not yet right to propose the application of Article K.9 [to asylum policy] so soon after the entry into force of the [TEU]" (Ibid:5-6).

While the issue of transfering asylum policy to the Community's competence thus remained in abeyance, intergovernmental discussions on asylum harmonization continued apace under the aegis of the K.4 Committee. In an effort to sidestep ratification and begin implementing various provisions of the Dublin Convention, the newly formed Steering Group I (Asylum/Immigration)—which replaced the Ad Hoc Immigration Group—recommended to the K.4 Committee that convention provisions pertaining to the transfer of asylum applicants be sent to the Council for approval (see K.4 Committee [SG I] 1993a).[69] Several days later, in a report to the JHA Council, the COREPER submitted draft conclusions on determining the means of proof required for identifying the member state responsible for examining an asylum application. Concerned that an overly rigid system of proof would penalize countries with more extensive national registers of asylum applications and burden the application examination process in general, the COREPER recommended that requirements be as streamlined as possible (see COREPER 1993b).

THE DECEMBER 1993 ACTION PLAN

On December 10, 1993, the Commission returned once more to the fray. It issued a Communication to the Council and the European Parliament containing two related recommendations for achieving progress on common border control and visa policy (Commission 1993c). The first proposal called for the elaboration and adoption of a **Convention on Controls on Persons Crossing External Frontiers** by December 31, 1994. This Convention was a revised version of the earlier draft External Frontiers Convention, and sought to salvage the principles already agreed upon by member states while incorporating the changes that had become necessary as a consequence of the TEU and the Agreement Establishing the European Economic Area (EAA).[70] Wary of the problems

---

[69] Belgium, Spain, and the Netherlands attached reservations to the recommendation. Belgium's reservation may have been the most troubling, as it related to that country's numerous Basque asylum claimants, an issue which brought to light the tension between political matters—i.e., whether an EU country could produce refugees—and the legal/judicial issue, which focused on whether, in fact, an asylum applicant may have been persecuted.

[70] In October 1991, EC and EFTA countries agreed to merge their free-trade zones into one European Economic Area. The **Agreement Establishing the European Economic Area (EEA)** was reached on May 2, 1992, and was scheduled to come into force by January 1, 1993. Although Switzerland was unable to ratify the Agreement after a national referendum in December 1992 rejected it, the EEA came into force January 1, 1994, after ratification by the eighteen remaining EC and EFTA countries. Once ratified, the EEA extended to the EFTA countries the EU's single-market legislation for removing all physical, fiscal, and technical barriers to trade. Although it does not entail the abolition of internal border controls,

already besetting the troubled EFC, the Commission insisted that any changes to the draft be "technical in character and confined to what is strictly necessary" (Ibid.:5) to prevent a further impasse on the Convention's signature and ratification. The proposal for the revised Convention was linked to a second proposal based on Article 100c, which called for a Council Resolution to establish a common list of third countries whose nationals would require a visa when crossing the external frontiers of the Community.

The Commission's recommendations were reflected in the action plan adopted by the Brussels Council on December 10-11, 1993. Immigration and asylum matters had always been considered in connection with other free-movement concerns such as drug trafficking, terrorism, and organized crime; the action plan formally linked these issues. The plan included the creation of a common visa list, increased efforts to combat illegal immigration, application of a comprehensive anti-drugs strategy, enhanced judicial cooperation (particularly with respect to extradition and international organized crime), and agreement on the principles to be used by member states in drafting bilateral or multilateral readmission agreements with third countries.[71] It also proposed that member states agree on: a uniform definition of "refugee" in accordance with Article 1A of the Geneva Convention, the immediate start-up of the Europol Drugs Unit, and the completion of the Europol Convention prior to October 1994 (see European Council 1993).

---

the EEA provides EFTA-country nationals with the same rights of entry and residence as EC nationals, thus requiring some modification of the draft EFC's visa provisions. Of even greater consequence for the draft EFC Convention, of course, was the entry into force of the Treaty on European Union, which granted the EC competence over visa policy (Article 100c).

[71] Cooperation with the countries of Central and Eastern Europe was deemed especially important in this regard, and would form the basis for another Berlin Conference meeting on September 8, 1994, attended by EU member states, Central and Eastern European countries, the United States, Canada, Switzerland, and Morocco. A **Recommendation concerning a specimen bilateral readmission agreement between a Member State of the European Union and a third country** was adopted by the JHA Council at its November 30–December 1, 1994 meeting. As noted by Bunyan and Webber (1995:21), the purpose of the recommendation was to "ensure identity of obligation among the periphery states forming a buffer zone around the European Union" by urging member states to negotiate with bordering countries conditions for automatically returning TCNs who transit through such countries without a valid visa. Similarly, the Recommendation urges that such accords include an agreement by these countries to accept their own nationals if these individuals are found to have entered—or are residing in—an EU country without valid documentation.

THE FEBRUARY 1994 COMMISSION COMMUNICATION

In February 1994, in an effort to capitalize on its TEU-granted right of initiative on third-pillar issue areas and to recapture the substantive and "idea-generating" ground it had gradually relinquished since the Maastricht Summit, the Commission unveiled a remarkably far-reaching **Communication to the Council and the European Parliament on Immigration and Asylum Polices** (see Commission 1994a). This Communication built on the ideas advanced in the October 1991 Communications, but went far beyond them in refining recommendations and more sharply defining the scope of proposed action. It was the most comprehensive blueprint yet of Commission thinking on immigration-related issues and sought to push the discussion beyond practical questions of harmonization toward renewed emphasis on long-term strategies to deal with immigration pressures as a whole.

The substance of the Communication elaborated on the new Community competencies in the immigration and asylum fields created by the TEU, and listed a series of recommendations for developing a "new framework for [Union] action" (Commission 1994a:41). It identified three key elements of a comprehensive approach:

(1) Reducing migration pressure, including measures to confront the "root causes" of migration;
(2) Controlling migration flows, including harmonization of general admission policies; and
(3) Strengthening integration policies for legal immigrants from third countries, particularly through measures granting them a uniform legal status.

Actions proposed under the first component—*reducing migration pressures*—included improvements in understanding the causes of migration. It identified measures needed to address root causes, such as "human rights policies; humanitarian assistance; security policy; demographic policies; trade, development, and cooperation policies; and [specified] exchange programs . . ." (Ibid:41). In addition, the Commission recommended the establishment of a migration "observatory" to improve data collection and monitoring of migration flows into the Union. Such an observatory would supplement Eurostat's and CIREA's data collection work in the area. In fact, the Commission proceeded to fund a full-scale feasibility study for such an observatory so that, should its recommendation be approved, the observatory could immediately become operational.

On the second component—controlling or, more accurately, *"managing" migration flows*—the Commission recommended: (a) completion of the general admission policies put forth in the December 1991 work program with regard to legally resident workers, self-employed persons, and students; (b) a draft convention on family reunification; and (c) harmonization of policies for admission on humanitarian grounds. On the latter, the Commission urged development of a common definition of "refugee" in accordance with Article 1A of the Geneva Convention (see fn. 100, p. 101 on the preliminary disposition of this matter); the drafting of conventions on manifestly unfounded asylum applications and implementation of the third-host-country principle; harmonization of temporary protection schemes; and development of a monitoring system for estimating and anticipating absorption capacities (Ibid:41-42).

The Commission made a number of recommendations to control unauthorized immigration. These included: (a) improved information exchanges on routes and carriers; (b) measures to combat illegal employment; (c) development of repatriation guidelines; (d) adoption and implementation of the revised draft External Frontiers Convention; and (e) the conclusion of readmission agreements with "safe" sending countries, including a linkage between such arrangements and the Community's external policies (Ibid.: 42-43).

The final component of the comprehensive approach—*integration policies*—focused on integrating legally resident third-country nationals. These included, *inter alia*: (a) harmonization of their legal status "with a view to ensuring a permanent residence entitlement"; (b) measures aimed at achieving TCN's free movement as workers within the Union; (c) efforts to remove member states' nationality criteria for the granting of rights and benefits to TCNs; (d) actions to reduce TCN unemployment; and (e) measures to combat racial discrimination and xenophobia (Ibid.:43-44).

In sum, the Communication offered a vision of managing immigration in Union territory through a combination of purposeful immigration regimes, improved interior and border controls, and a more enlightened and longer-term emphasis on addressing emigration's root causes as a means of reducing migration pressure. It also forcefully sought to reopen discussions—however narrowly—about the status of TCNs legally resident in the Union.

As important as all these recommendations are, the most consequential aspect of the February 1994 Communication may have been the Commission's bid to regain its place as the moral and visionary voice of Europe. In an important passage, the Commission observed:

[I]t has long been recognized that immigration is not a temporary phenomenon . . . . [Earlier] assumptions to that effect . . . were based on fundamental misconceptions as to the nature of immigration patterns which became established in the post-war period. More importantly, immigration has been a positive process which has brought economic and broader cultural benefits both to the host countries and the immigrants themselves. Some have called for a complete halt to immigration: *this is neither feasible nor desirable*. What is necessary is proper management of immigration policy. The Community has *always been a multi-cultural and multi-ethnic entity* whose diversity enriches the Community itself and benefits all its citizens, but not without creating challenges for society as a whole and its immigrant communities (Ibid.:1; emphasis added).

ADDRESSING ROOT CAUSES

For the long term, the most important recommendation in the February 1994 Communication was perhaps its push to link the broader management of migration pressures with the Union's *foreign policy* agenda, especially development assistance and economic cooperation with third countries. This recognized the need to look beyond provisions for controlling admission to "preventive" measures that would encourage immigrants to stay in their countries of origin.

Some analysts are disconcerted by the tone of the Union's "root causes" discussions, charging that it is primarily defensive and analogous to other exclusionary rhetoric.[72] Even critics

---

[72] Collinson, for example, makes a perhaps unnecessarily stark but nonetheless important observation about the Union's linkage of root causes and immigration restrictions and controls: "Action to tackle the root causes," she argues, "is treated as another 'solution' to the migration 'problem,' and is therefore as reactive in its basis as action to strengthen immigration controls . . . . Such . . . [a] blanket approach to prevention misses the complexity of . . . [immigration] and is thus unlikely to be adequately responsive to the questions and challenges raised by it" (1994:55, 57).

acknowledge that a "root causes" approach has long-term value as a tool for both development and stemming migration. But in the short and medium term, there is reason to be skeptical. First, the development process is more likely to aggravate emigration pressures for a period of time than to arrest them (see Papademetriou 1994 and U.S. Commission 1990). Second, a *sustained* effort to attack root causes requires enormous amounts of physical and political capital, as well as extraordinary clarity of purpose and unequaled policy and political coordination within and among governments. Finally, the most immediate and politically unsustainable immigration flows have been caused by intra-regional conflict (largely on Europe's immediate eastern and southern periphery), not by overpopulation and underdevelopment in the South.

The root-causes approach to immigration was the subject of several subsequent meetings. At an informal meeting in Thessaloniki, Greece, in May 1994, Ministers of the Interior discussed possible cooperation on data collection regarding the situation in sending countries and "socio-economic intervention" to confront the origins of migration pressure. They concluded with a statement acknowledging the need to devise a "global approach [to immigration that] moved beyond the third pillar" of the Union (European Ministers of the Interior 1994:3).[73]

Soon afterward, at the request of the Greek Presidency, the Commission agreed to finance a conference to consider the possibilities for establishing a "root causes" approach. Held in June 1994 in Vouliagmeni, outside Athens, the conference reached consensus on the need to link the Union's immigration and foreign policies. However, participants—immigration experts and policy officials—agreed that assigning priority to policies on root causes would require "political courage" on the part of member states, because the effects would "only be noticeable in the long run" (Commission 1994e:1).[74]

---

[73] The Ministers also analyzed the problems of temporary protection and absorption (including the need to investigate possible solutions short of asylum), as well as measures to combat illegal immigration.

[74] The Conference also noted that, while the Commission's Communication had received attention by the JHA Council (and the Social and Development Councils), it had not yet been the subject of any "substantive discussion" of the General Affairs Council, the body responsible for Community foreign policy matters (see Commission 1994e:8).

INTERGOVERNMENTAL INSTITUTIONS REASSERT
PRIMACY ON IMMIGRATION AND ASYLUM

At the JHA Council's March 23 meeting, initial reactions to the February Communication were tepid at best—in effect raising questions once more about the Commission's timing and instincts. Noting that the Communication could serve as "a good basis for future reflection" (JHA Council 1994b:2), the Council nevertheless urged continued efforts to implement the narrower work program agreed upon in December 1993. As for the Commission's recommendations to develop a comprehensive immigration policy, the Council agreed merely to instruct the COREPER to work with the K.4 Committee "to decide on the bodies responsible for examining the various aspects of the Communication" (Ibid:3).

Meeting in Luxembourg in June 1994, the JHA Council continued with its own agenda of immigration management and control; it adopted the **Resolution on Limitations on Admission of [TCNs] to the Member States for Employment** (see JHA Council 1994c).[75] The Resolution noted that, although migrant workers had contributed to the economic development of host countries, present levels of unemployment in member states increased the need "to bring Community employment preference properly into place" (Ibid:12). It added that it was necessary to restrict admission to Union territory for employment reasons, noting that "no Member State [was] pursuing an active immigration policy . . . [but] on the contrary . . . [all] had] curtailed the possibility of permanent legal immigration for economic, social, and thus political reasons" (Ibid.).

The Resolution stipulated that member states should employ non-EU or non-EFTA nationals only when they are unable to find EU, EFTA, or long-term resident TCN workers to fill a position. But it also included provisions allowing temporary labor recruitment under specified conditions (e.g., intra-firm employee transfers, seasonal employment, and to fill labor shortages). In recognition of the many bilateral employment, training, and worker-exchange agreements to which member states were parties, the JHA Council exempted them from the Resolution's reach. In other words,

---

[75] A draft of this resolution had been submitted by the Ad Hoc Immigration Group to the Immigration Ministers at the November 30–December 1, 1992 meeting, to correspond with objectives put forth in the December 1991 work program. Final approval of the resolution was held up by various amendments to the original draft.

rhetoric notwithstanding, the Resolution continued to permit the employment of foreigners for virtually all the reasons EU states generally recruit and employ foreign- born individuals.

In December 1994, the JHA Council agreed on two additional resolutions. The **Resolution relating to limitations on the admission of [TCNs] to the territory of the Member States for the purpose of pursuing activities as self-employed persons** recognized the positive contribution of self-employed TCNs to the host economies; it created a special category of "service providers" who would be admitted to a member state for a specified period. It also recommended a number of checks to ensure that self-employed TCNs do not accept payroll employment in the region (see Council 1994l). The **Resolution on the admission of [TCNs] to the territory . . . for study purposes** similarly recognized the benefits of international student exchanges, while recommending measures to prevent students from remaining in the country after their studies are completed (see COREPER 1994h). Both resolutions allow such entrants to be accompanied by family members. Except for the Resolution on foreign students, the other two resolutions were careful to allow member states to meet their obligations under the General Agreement on Trade in Services (GATS), a key component of the Uruguay Round of the General Agreement on Tariffs and Trade (GATT).

THE COMMISSION AGENDA RESURFACES

Despite the Council's decision to reassert the primacy of an intergovernmental approach, it would be inaccurate to suggest that the Commission's February 1994 Communication has had no resonance. For instance, while immigration is not formally a common agenda item, it is beginning to be recognized as such by other Commission structures, particularly those dealing with trade and development issues. Furthermore, the lexicon of "root causes" and of the importance of a "global approach" to immigration continues to be embraced and elaborated, if often only rhetorically.

COMBATING RACISM AND XENOPHOBIA

Another aspect of the February 1994 Communication—the importance of strengthening the social integration of legal immigrants—has not gone altogether unheeded. Alarmed at the incidence of "hate" crimes in their countries, France and Germany successfully proposed the creation of a Union-level Consultative Commission at the June 1994 Corfu Summit. The Consultative Commission was charged with generating recommendations on cooperative public and private-sector measures that would encourage "tolerance and understanding of foreigners" and with developing a global strategy "aimed at combating acts of racist and global violence" (European Council 1994a:134-135).[76]

In its report to the COREPER and the General Affairs Council in the spring of 1995, the Consultative Committee recommended that the Community be given competence to combat racism and xenophobia. It also recommended that the Community define more precisely what constitutes a racist or xenophobic act, improve data collection on race-related or hate crimes, and improve cross-border cooperation and information exchanges between enforcement bodies.

In response to these recommendations, EU Social Affairs Commissioner Padraig Flynn announced that the Commission intended to push for competence in this area under the next revision of the Rome Treaty. Stating that such measures are necessary to achieve freedom of movement for all workers, Flynn argued for Commission intervention in matters pertaining to immigrant education and integration, the prevention of discrimination, and the curtailment of anti-immigrant propaganda. The Commission also proposed the establishment of a **European Observatory on Racism and Xenophobia** responsible for coordinating public and private efforts against racism and xenophobia at the European and international level, and recommended that Europol's mandate be expanded to include combating racism and xenophobia (*Migration News Sheet* 1995d:8).

The Union's activism on this issue culminated in a Consultative Commission proposal for a **Joint Action on Racism and Xenophobia**, presented to the JHA Council in November 1995. The Joint Action calls on national police forces and judicial authorities to cooperate (initially until the mid-1997) in fighting the dissemination of racist and xenophobic literature and the activities of racist groups (see *Financial Times* 1995h:2). The JHA Council was

---

[76] One of the earliest efforts in this regard was the adoption by the European Parliament, the Council, and the Commission of a **Joint Declaration Against Racism and Xenophobia** in 1986 (see Commission 1993a: Annex II).

unable to adopt the Joint Action proposal because of U.K. objections, which included the by-now standard issue of "competence," British sensitivity about outside interference with or criticism of its race relations record, and philosophical differences on the issue of censorship that reflect the differing judicial and civil liberties traditions of the United Kingdom and those of other European member states.[77]

INTEGRATION AND TCN RIGHTS: FORGOTTEN AGENDAS?

Even as significant progress was being made on the anti-racism and anti-xenophobia front, the issue of integration of TCNs continued to challenge the Union. Continuing with its attempt to resolve the issue, the Commission issued a **White Paper on European Social Policy** in July 1994, in which it reiterated its conviction that integration of TCNs is an indispensable component of fuller Union integration. The Commission stated that the free movement of persons "logically implies the free movement of all legally resident third country nationals for the purpose of engaging in economic activities" (Commission 1994f:39), and it urged that integration policies go further "towards strengthening [TCNs'] rights relative to those of citizens of the Member States" (Ibid:38). In April 1995, the Commission followed up with a detailed three-year **Social Action Programme** outlining, among other things, its intention to push for the further integration of TCNs and announcing its plan to draft a recommendation encouraging member states to adopt the 1990 U.N. International Convention on the Protection of the Rights of Migrant Workers and their Families (see Commission 1995:24-25).

RECENT PRESIDENCIES: TOWARD A "EUROPE OF TWO SPEEDS?"

THE GERMAN PRESIDENCY

At the beginning of its tenure in July 1994, the German Presidency signaled that it would not press strongly for a comprehensive reso-

---

[77] Under U.K. law, the act of disseminating hate and other objectionable material is not prohibited unless the *intent* behind that act is to incite actions that are criminally sanctionable. The Joint Action proposal ignores that critical distinction and would necessitate a change in British law.

lution of the impasse on immigration matters. Rather, it would adhere closely to the priorities set by the Council in its December 1993 action plan: establishment of minimum procedural guarantees for examining asylum applications; visa-policy harmonization[78]; proposals for revising the draft External Frontiers Convention in light of the entry into force of the TEU and the European Economic Area Agreement; efforts to curb illegal immigration, including upgrading CIREFI from an information-and-discussion center to an operational agency[79]; admission of self-employed persons and students from third countries[80]; and common expulsion measures (see JHA Council 1993b).

Nevertheless, Germany has long been a proponent of a more "federal" Europe. Although its focus on immigration matters was narrower than the Commission's, the German Presidency made clear its hope that third-pillar issues would be brought gradually into the competence of the EU—a view it had maintained steadily since the Luxembourg Summit of June 1991. This view was reflected in the boldly worded "Lamers Report" (so named after its author, Karl Lamers)—a set of "reflections on European policy" published in September 1994 by Chancellor Kohl's Christian Democratic Union (CDU) in anticipation of the 1996 Intergovernmental Conference. The Lamers Report put forth a vision of federal Europe. The report offered a "solution" to the ongoing dispute among member states over the depth and pace of Union integration, advocating that a central core of states committed to greater integration and closer cooperation forge ahead with political and economic union, while states seeking a less federal structure continue cooperating with the Union through a separate intergovernmental framework.[81] Under this "two-speed" system of European

---

[78] Exercising its authority under Article 100c, the Commission submitted a proposal for the introduction of a common visa format in August 1994, which went to the European Parliament for an opinion.

[79] Beginning in January 1995, a monthly conference has been convened within CIREFI to address issues aimed at preventing unauthorized immigration and illegal residence, combating immigration crime, detecting forged documents, and improving expulsion procedures.

[80] A draft resolution on this subject was submitted by the German Presidency to the Council on July 1, 1994 (see also the Resolution passed by the JHA Council in December 1994, discussed on pp. 88).

[81] In this plan, the Council of Ministers and European Parliament would comprise a two-chamber legislature in the new "federal state," with the Commission possessing characteristics of a "European government."

integration, the third pillar would be dissolved and its responsibilities turned over to the Union's central institutions, which would oversee such issues as the harmonization of asylum and refugee policies, refugee "burden-sharing" among member states, and the establishment of Europol (see *Financial Times* 1995a:2, and 1995b:15).

When the Lamers Report met with negative reactions from several member states, notably the United Kingdom and France, the German government modified the proposal before re-releasing it in June 1995. This more chastened document omitted any reference to a "core" group of European member states and called for increased efficiency within—rather than the dissolution of—the intergovernmental pillar framework.

Meanwhile, the ambitious goals of the German Presidency with regard to the December 1993 action plan fell far short of its own expectations. Distracted by an electoral jamboree[82] that ended in national elections in October 1994, Germany had relatively little progress to report at the Essen Summit that December. Beyond a valedictory on the accomplishments of Commission President Jacques Delors,[83] the Summit focused primarily on preparations for the accession of new member states (Austria, Finland, and Sweden[84]) and, more controversially, on the eventual addition of the Union's eastern neighbors.[85]

The Essen Council nonetheless went on to note the "progress" already achieved toward harmonization in asylum law, visa policy, and criteria for admitting students and self-employed individuals. It did so while urging that a number of outstanding

---

[82] Most German states (Länder) held elections in 1994. The elections for the European Parliament also took place that year (June).

[83] Delors was praised for "the ten most successful years of European unification" including his role in directing the Single European Act, the completion of the internal market, and progress toward economic and monetary union (see European Council 1994b:140).

[84] Norway, the other EFTA country that had applied to join the Union, rejected EU membership in a national referendum in November 1994.

[85] The Council examined this matter in an unusual set of meetings with the heads of state and government (and the foreign ministers) of Bulgaria, the Czech Republic, Hungary, Poland, Romania, and the Slovak Republic. It noted, however, that "the institutional conditions for ensuring the proper functioning of the Union," the main topic of the 1996 Intergovernmental Conference, had to be resolved *before* accession negotiations could begin (European Council 1994b:145).

matters—e.g., the list of third countries subject to visa requirements, creation of a uniform visa, and finalization of the Europol
Convention—be completed by the June 1995 Cannes Summit. The
German Presidency attached great importance to the Europol Convention, as evidenced by the 30 days of meetings it devoted to this
effort. At the Essen Summit, Chancellor Kohl, supported by Italy
and the Benelux countries, convinced then-President Mitterand of
France to commit to completing work on the Convention by the
June 1995 Summit (Vos 1995).

Freedom of movement issues were also discussed at Essen
within the broader context of "Europe and its citizens." In addition
to asserting yet again that the Union "must become more transpar-
ent and closer to its citizens" (European Council 1994b:150), the
Council recommended that the revised External Frontiers Convention be concluded and submitted for signature prior to the Cannes
meeting.[86]

The Council emphasized the importance of the "Union-wide
fight against racism and xenophobia" (Ibid.:151) and approved the
guidelines in the Consultative Commission's report. Finally, the
Council paid "tribute" to the preparations taken by member states
to *temporarily* admit large groups of refugees from war and civil
war. At the same time, it called upon the JHA ministers to study the
problems this might create for EU member states in order to find
"an effective arrangement for future sharing of the burden of
humanitarian assistance" (Ibid.:150).

DOMESTIC POLITICS AND THE FRENCH PRESIDENCY

When Germany's Presidency term ended, France took over.
France was then in the throes of a volatile national campaign sea-
son that eventually led to the election of the neo-Gaullist President, Jacques Chirac. France had always been a crucial swing
state in the face-off between Germany and the United Kingdom
over the direction of Europe. Preoccupied with domestic politics,

---

[86] However, the dispute between the United Kingdom and Spain over Gibraltar
remained unresolved. EU Commissioner Padraig Flynn stated as much in a speech on
December 1, 1994, in the wake of numerous complaints lodged by Spain over the smuggling of drugs, cigarettes, and other contraband items through Gibraltar (see *Migration
News Sheet*,1995a:1).

the French Presidency helped to slow integration momentum by forcing the Commission to take a back seat in Community matters, while catering to the nationalist—and occasionally xenophobic—strains in the French electorate (see Papademetriou and Hamilton 1996).

Partly for this reason, the French Presidency reflected—and intensified—the Union's continuing preoccupation with controls. In early 1995, it forwarded an agenda focusing on combating the unauthorized immigration and employment of foreign nationals, coordinating the status of asylum seekers and refugees (with an eye to implementing the Dublin Convention), and creating a common visa policy. The Council considered two draft regulations on visa policy. The first pertained to the long-standing effort to develop a common "negative list" of countries whose nationals would require a visa to enter Union space—an attempt to move forward on establishing common admission criteria without waiting for the External Frontiers Convention. The list prepared by the Commission covered 126 countries. However, the United Kingdom objected to including British Commonwealth countries, whose nationals enjoy visa-free travel to the United Kingdom, and counter-proposed that only 74 countries be included on the list. Similarly, Italy opposed inclusion of Serbia and Montenegro on the list. Thus final agreement was blocked.[87]

The second visa proposal under consideration during the French Presidency concerned the development of a common visa format. This proposal suffered a setback during the March 1995 meeting of Interior Ministers, when Conservative "Euro-skeptics" in the British Parliament persuaded Prime Minister Major's government to delay agreement subject to a House of Commons debate. The Tory "rebels" likened the mutual recognition of visas to relaxing internal border controls—another move, in their view, toward the "slippery slope" of establishing a federal Europe. JHA Ministers did reach agreement, however, on a **Convention on simplified extradition**, the first convention to be adopted within the third-pillar framework.

The French Presidency had announced its intention to focus on harmonizing the status of long-term legally resident TCNs. It

---

[87] According to Article K.9 of the TEU, agreement must be reached by unanimity until January 1, 1996—after which only a qualified majority is required.

proposed a joint action establishing a single residence and work permit which, among other things, would have allowed TCNs to move to other member states for employment. The JHA Council was unable to reach agreement on the final text of this proposal at its June 20-21, 1995, meeting, however, and the subsequent Spanish Presidency (July through December 1995) also was unable to make progress. If and when approved and adopted, such an initiative would constitute an important and long-overdue development regarding free-movement rights for TCNs in the EU.

The JHA Council also failed to approve a French proposal for a joint action to establish a common approach to illegal immigration and unauthorized employment. In this case, member states objected not so much to the proposal's contents as to the obligations they would incur because it was a "joint action." They did, however, agree to adopt it as a much less demanding "recommendation." The Ministers also agreed on a **Resolution on minimum guarantees for asylum proceedings**, which provided protection guarantees for refugees in accordance with the provisions of the 1951 Geneva Convention. These guarantees included an asylum applicant's right to appeal a negative decision to an independent authority, to have applications described in a language that he or she understands, and to have a personal interview before a final decision is made. These conditions did not, however, apply in "manifestly unfounded" cases or cases where applicants had transited through a "safe" or "safe third" country (see Council 1994h).

"SCHENGENLAND"

Nowhere has the dominance of domestic priorities over broadly defined "Community" interests been more apparent than in the shifting French views toward the Schengen Agreement. The scheduled full implementation of the Agreement by July 1, 1995, was to have been one of the more significant achievements during the French Presidency—albeit one that would have occurred independently of EU processes. On March 26, 1995, a three-month trial period began as scheduled. Henceforth, nationals of the seven member countries—France, Germany, Spain, Portugal, and the Benelux countries—could move virtually check-free within the new "Schengenland," and TCNs who entered any one of the Schengen states were permitted to travel to the other Schengen states without additional document checks.[88] In a reluctant concession to the French government, which was in the midst of both presidential and municipal election campaigns in late spring and early summer,[89] some checks were maintained at the internal borders of Schengen states during the trial period.

The implementation of Schengen has received mixed reviews. Satisfaction over greater freedom of movement has vied with heightened apprehensions over illegal immigration and cross-border crime. In addition, some Schengen states have begun to express dissatisfaction with the way other member states are implementing the Agreement. France, for instance, complains that the "soft" drugs policy of the Netherlands is promoting increased drug trafficking within the region; it also contends that Spain's and Portugal's insufficient data processing on criminals threatens the operation and accuracy of the Schengen Information System police data base. Germany has protested that Italy—which has not yet ratified the Agreement—has been allowing nationals from Serbia and Montenegro (countries on Schengen's "negative list") visa-free entry, while also admitting hundreds of *illegal* immigrants from these countries, Albania, and Turkey (*Migration News Sheet* 1995c:2). Germany and Belgium have condemned France's lack of cooperation in police pursuits of criminals across the French border.

The Agreement has also created a number of more technical problems. For instance, tightened frontier checks at Germany's

---

[88] This was already happening in practice at the Schengen member states' land borders. With the implementation of the Agreement, it took place at airports as well, as flights to other Schengen countries were now treated as domestic, rather than international flights. The refusal of some countries (such as the United Kingdom) to join Schengen, and the inability of others (such as Italy) to do so because of inadequate preparations (see Papademetriou and Hamilton 1996) continue to be obstacles to Schengen's wider adoption. Other countries, such as Norway and Iceland, are interested in participating but are unable to do so (as EU non-members). This has raised problems for yet another group of EU member states (such as Finland and Sweden) who would like to join but do not wish to give up their visa-free arrangements with the two other countries (Norway and Iceland) who are members of the 40-year-old Nordic Passport Union.

[89] The campaign in France was especially unsteady, with far-right candidate Jean Marie Le Pen (of the National Front, or FN) hoping to translate growing racial and ethnic tensions toward legal and illegal foreign residents, as well as more generalized anti-government sentiment, into electoral success. Le Pen's ability to win 15 percent of the votes in the first-round ballot on April 23 left both Socialist and Gaullist candidates fearful of even greater FN gains in the country's upcoming municipal elections. Not wanting to appear soft on border control matters, the new Chirac government was forced to tread carefully on the matter so as not to alienate an already disgruntled French public (see Papademetriou and Hamilton 1996).

eastern border with Poland have resulted in huge waiting lines that threaten Germany's business relations with its important trading partners to the east; Amsterdam's Schiphol airport reintroduced passport checks after the airport's infrastructure proved inefficient in distinguishing between Schengen and non-Schengen passengers.

France has proven to be the biggest obstacle to full implementation of Schengen. On May 2, 1995, shortly after the election demonstrated growing support for the right-wing National Front, France reintroduced checks at its frontiers with other Schengen states. Then, on June 28, on the eve of the scheduled final implementation of the Agreement, France announced that it would invoke the safeguard clause (Article 2, Paragraph 2) for a six-month period, until the remaining implementation problems had been resolved. This announcement infuriated fellow Schengen member states, who vowed to press ahead without France after the six-month period.[90]

Furthermore, other countries continue to express interest in joining Schengen. In June, Schengen and Nordic state ministers met to discuss the terms under which Denmark, Finland, and Sweden might participate in Schengen without infringing on their free-movement agreements with non-EU Nordic states Iceland and Norway (*Migration News Sheet* 1995c:3).[91] Under the agreement reached, Iceland and Norway were granted associate membership, which requires them to adapt their visa, immigration, and asylum policies to those of the Schengen states, although it does not extend Schengen's free movement provisions to their nationals.

Schengen provides both a challenge and an opportunity for EU member states. The challenge for a core set of EU countries is to overcome the Union's inability to implement measures they consider essential to the realization of a single Europe. At the same time, Schengen serves as a test case—offering other EU members the opportunity to observe, learn from, and (if it is successful) eventually emulate—while also making the Union's failure to approve the External Frontiers Convention less consequential and further isolating the United Kingdom.

---

[90] In January 1996 the French quitely reentered the Schengen mainstream in all regards except those involving traffic from the Netherlands.

[91] See also *supra* fn. 88, p. 96. Finland had applied for observer status with Schengen on May 5, 1995 with Sweden following suit on June 15.

THE JUNE 1995 CANNES SUMMIT

The first Council of the Fifteen convened on June 26-27, 1995, in Cannes, France. Eleven additional candidates for EU membership (Bulgaria, Cyprus, the Czech Republic, Estonia, Hungary, Latvia, Lithuania, Malta, Poland, Romania, and the Slovak Republic) also attended some of the meetings. As in several previous summits, domestic politics played a prominent role and served to highlight the seemingly irreparable fissure among EU member states over the future direction of Europe.[92]

One of the most notable "casualties" of the French Summit was the **Europol Convention**. Although member states agreed on most of its principles, they deadlocked once again over the issue of whether the European Court of Justice should have the authority to adjudicate disputes arising from the Convention's implementation. The United Kingdom insisted—as it had on most matters of first-pillar competence—that sensitive matters such as crime be handled exclusively on a government–to–government basis and objected to any extension of ECJ authority into matters relating to international conventions. The Benelux countries, particularly the Netherlands, refused to acquiesce to the U.K. position, arguing that ECJ competence is necessary to ensure the Convention's uniform application and to guarantee EU citizens' rights to be heard before an independent court. Member states agreed to sign the Convention (on July 26, 1995) but to postpone final decision on the matter of ECJ competence until June 1996. The Benelux countries vowed not to ratify Europol until a satisfactory solution is found. Germany, Italy, and Austria have also urged resolution of the dispute. Until a final decision is reached, Europol will assume a much narrower role than originally envisioned on issues such as drugs, money laundering, car theft, and illegal immigration.

The quarrel over Europol[93] was only one of a number of setbacks at the Cannes Summit. Postponements on European monetary

---

[92] British Prime Minister John Major arrived at the Summit having resigned as leader of his Conservative Party a few days earlier after a revolt within the Party over the direction of Europe. As for the new French government, other member states sought to gauge the depth and direction of President Chirac's commitment to Europe by observing where he positioned himself among the divergent views most prominently represented by Germany and the United Kingdom.

[93] As of this writing, the impasse has not been resolved, and the rhetoric of the key antagonists—the United Kingdom and the Netherlands—has not changed.

integration and arguments over majority voting on foreign-policy decisions added to an already somber mood about further integration. Throughout the deliberations, it was not clear where France would side in the debate between the United Kingdom and Germany over the direction of Europe. At the closing dinner, President Chirac pronounced that the "nation-state in Europe is not dead" and urged that the European Commission be kept on a tight leash. Legitimacy for European decisions, he insisted, rested with the intergovernmental Council. Chirac's rhetoric[94] and Britain's recalcitrance fueled concerns that a rising tide of populist nationalism would continue to thwart efforts toward further integration.

In early July, the Commission, apparently unfazed by this climate of pessimism, unveiled proposals for the final elimination of border controls between member states. The Commission had been completely reformulated in January 1995. While many once again questioned its motives,[95] political instincts, and timing, the Commission defended its actions by reiterating its usual argument that a frontier-free space was necessary for the creation of a "citizens' Europe" that provides for free movement of persons, as well as goods, services, and capital. It also attempted to allay fears that such a move would lead to a flood of illegal immigrants by insisting that external checks would be strengthened and in place before any member state would be asked to relinquish control over its borders.[96] Not surprisingly, the proposal was immediately shot down by the United Kingdom, which announced on July 12 that it would veto the measure.

EFFECTS ON THE UNION'S CENTRAL INSTITUTIONS

Schengen, the Cannes Summit, and decisions taken during the ensuing Spanish Presidency on the timing and requirements for

---

[94] Although some of the French government stances on these issues would "soften" and come much closer to the German viewpoint—*particularly on issues relating to French participation in the Economic and Monetary Union (EMU) as a charter member*—French reluctance to surrender competence to the Union has continued as a matter of principle.

[95] There is some speculation that the Commission's decision to push ahead despite the hostile climate was an effort to preempt a ruling by the European Court of Justice on a case brought against it two years earlier by the European Parliament for failing to implement the Single European Act.

[96] The Commission sought to bolster its argument by noting that, contrary to popular perceptions, most illegal immigrants entered Union space legally and over-stayed their visas. Furthermore, it contended, systematic border controls had rarely intercepted drug traffickers, terrorists, or other criminals.

acceding to the Economic and Monetary Union[97] may yet come to represent the "Europe of two speeds" envisioned in the Lamers Report. If this occurs, the Commission's ability to pursue ambitious new initiatives *effectively*[98] in most of the areas discussed in this essay will continue to be heavily circumscribed. This can be attributed to several factors, including the loss of momentum when a new management team was selected and installed in the Commission, the need to accommodate new members (Austria, Sweden, and Finland) in the EU, and sheer exhaustion after the breakneck pace—and breadth—of the Union's agenda once the TEU came into force. These same factors will test the ability of other Union institutions (as well as national institutions) to reach closure on all but a handful of key agenda items—even those on which substantial progress already has been made.

Similarly, the experience with immigration and asylum issues highlights problems in the institutional processes and procedures created by the TEU. In hindsight, it is obvious to practitioners and observers alike that Union procedures will have to be streamlined further if the Community is to function with its increased membership. At a minimum, such streamlining must include rethinking the pillars structure and the multi-step procedures for channeling matters to the Union's decision-making bodies (i.e., the various EU Councils), reorganizing and even paring down an unwieldy Commission, and extending majority voting to more issue areas.

WILL THE UNION HOLD?

Dissatisfaction with the Community's pillar structure is nearly universal. In May 1995, the Commission released its own critique of TEU procedures, in particular the "incoherence" created by the co-existing operation of two different working methods—

---

[97] It now appears that the EMU will be launched on time in 1999 and without any changes in the stringent economic performance requirements originally agreed upon. See *Washington Post* 1995a:32; *The European* 1995a, 1995b, 1995c; and *The Economist* 1995a, 1995b, 1995c.

[98] The measure of the effectiveness of the Commission necessarily lies in the actual *adoption* of a least the basic thrust of its proposals and recommendations.

the Community approach and the intergovernmental approach—within the same Treaty (*Migration News Sheet* 1995b:1). The Commission was particularly critical of the intergovernmental JHA third pillar, charging that its "unanimity requirements" were the single most important source of inefficiency and "paralysis" in Community action—as made evident by the nine conventions that have yet to come to closure.[99] A Council report made some of the same criticisms, citing as particularly "cumbersome" the five-layer structure of the third pillar, with its working parties, steering groups, the K.4 Committee, COREPER, and the Council of Ministers (Ibid.:1). These criticisms, together with frustration over the failure to reach an acceptable agreement on the Europol Convention—an area in which members concur that cooperation is necessary—foreshadows a protracted debate over the efficacy of the Union's third pillar, inter-pillar relationships, and possibly also horizontal cooperation among European institutions at the Intergovernmental Conference scheduled to start in late March of 1996 and expected to last until at least mid-1997.[100]

Preliminary reports from the Reflection Group,[101] the intergovernmental body responsible for preparing the blueprint for the IGC's deliberations, give a sense of the enormity—and, given the record to date, the unreasonableness—of the task the IGC will

---

[99] One notable exception to this remarkable lack of closure on substantive matters may be a pending JHA Council "joint position" on the application of the term "refugee" in Article 1A of the 1951 Geneva Convention. As of this writing, the text had not been finalized. It appears, however, that the agreement's definition of a refugee would be narrower than that used by virtually every EU member state—most notably leaving "unprotected" those fleeing persecution by non-state organizations or escaping civil war. The tentative agreement has been denounced by refugee advocates and has earned expressions of concern by the U.N. High Commissioner for Refugees (UNHCR) for its restrictive interpretation of the 1951 Convention. (The High Commissioner's office also welcomed certain provisions, however, such as the agreement's commitment to continue to examine all claims individually.) Although the text will be binding when formally approved, it would explicitly allow decisions taken in national courts—which are typically more liberal than those taken by administrators—to be implemented regardless of their conformity with the agreement (JHA Council 1995b and *Financial Times* 1995f:2).

[100] The initial impetus for a 1996 Treaty review came from Germany, which was dissatisfied with the compromises on political union at the Maastricht Summit.

[101] The Reflection Group is comprised of representatives of the fifteen member states. It was launched on June 2, 1995, in Messina, Italy, on the fortieth anniversary and site of the 1955 conference that laid the foundation for the original Treaty of Rome.

face. In addition to the difficult issues relating to institutional reforms,[102] and to common foreign and defense policies[103] (a German-French priority that is beyond the scope of this essay), the IGC will also have to revisit the many difficult "democratization" issues left unresolved at Maastricht. These include granting more powers to the European Parliament,[104] moving to weighted majority voting in the Council on a variety of issues (a reform that has become more essential as the Union has grown), transfering competence on many JHA issues to the Commission, and opening up the deliberations of the Council to more public scrutiny. In addition, it will need to devise a formula, if only in principle, for reforming the deeply entrenched agricultural and regional development policies that absorb about three-quarters of the Union's budget[105]—while at the same time preparing for the Union's fur-

---

[102] "Institutional reforms" must go beyond reconsidering or fine-tuning the Union's pillar structure to addressing the following fundamental issues: whether the institutional framework devised to handle a limited number of functions and initially involving only six countries can adequately perform the multitude of tasks required of a single market and handle the complex interrelationships of a fifteen-member entity that seems committed to further enlargement.

[103] Economic and monetary union (EMU) has been left deliberately outside of the purview of the IGC in an attempt to punctuate that both EMU and its timetables are non-negotiable.

[104] Granting the European Parliament (EP) additional powers so as to force more sunshine into and greater scrutiny of the Union's actions now commands the status of mantra. Before the IGC invests too much energy on this issue, however, it must be clear about two points: First, is the cause of openess and democracy best served by a stronger EP or should the organizational structure of that institution (see box **2-1**, p. 8) also be reconsidered? Second, could additional measures that open and institutionalize channels of communications between the European Parliament and national parliaments (where openess is the greatest) be an additional avenue for responding to the Union's "democratic-deficit" problems. The devolution of power from central to state and local governmental institutions that has been sweeping the advanced democracies—a process the United States calls "federalism" and one that is quite consistent with the EU principle of "subsidiarity" (see fn. 114, p. 110)—suggests that measures other than concentrating powers should considered.

[105] These policies, however badly in need of reform, are virtually "non-negotiable" for their main beneficiaries—Greece, Ireland, Portugal, and Spain. Yet, unless Europe's economies recover dramatically by 1999, when the present budget agreement expires, and if the Union continues to fail to establish its relevance to important concerns of Europe's publics, the budget issue may prove to be one of the Union's most intractable problems. In such a scenario, many member states may find themselves hard-pressed to explain to their electorates why some of their taxes must go to Brussels to support goals and activities over which they have little say and even less control—and which they understand very imperfectly—at the same time that their governments are cutting back their own social benefits.

ther enlargement[106] and for meeting the commitments it has made to the countries of the southern Mediterranean.[107]

As if this agenda were not intimidating enough, the IGC must also come to terms with the growing rift between the so-called "fundamentalists" (the federalist-leaning Benelux countries and frequently Germany) and the constantly shifting coalitions of other member states on most issues (see *Economist* 1995d:53). This was plainly evident in the deliberations of the Reflection Group, where the U.K. representative consistently reiterated Britain's desire for a more loosely structured Union, with less centralized decision-making and greater flexibility to "opt out." Britain has threatened to veto any extension of majority voting at the IGC, for example.[108] The more federalist-minded states, for their part, fear that any relaxation in Community obligations and structures will drastically weaken the Union, turning it into little more than a free-trade zone.

As Europe has the opportunity once again to devise a new identity for itself and to reconsider some of its structures and their functions, it is extraordinary just how elusive the vision of Maastricht has been. The story of attempts to harmonize Union policy on immigration, refugee, and asylum matters is in some ways both cause and effect of the entrenched—and, at present, probably irreconcilable—differences over the direction of Europe. This is not the first time, however, that Europe has faced a break in momentum. It is quite possible that with a new vision, scaled-back expectations, and rethought—and refined—roles for its institutions, Europe's integration agenda can again move forward.

---

[106] Toward the end of the Spanish Presidency, it appeared that German insistence on quick accession by some Eastern European countries would fail to overcome French and most other EU member states' resistance both to moving forward too fast and to showing preference on who should accede first. As a result, although accession negotiations may start in some instances as early as 1997, the expectation is that they will be protracted, that the requirements for accession will be applied with rigor, and that the transition period for full membership in most instances will be quite long (see *International Herald Tribune* 1995:5 and *Financial Times* 1995e:17).

[107] In an event of potentially historic significance, the EU met for three days in November with the states of the southern rim of the Mediterranean littoral and committed to forming free trade areas with them by 2010 (see *Christian Science Monitor* 1995:6 and *Financial Times* 1995g:4).

[108] It is not preordained that British general elections in the spring 1996 will lead to a reversal of British intransigence on most competence issues—even if a Labor government emerges. There are relatively few differences between the Tories and Labor on most Justice and Home Affairs issues, and the Tories' recent nationalist proclivities are echoed by many in the Labor Party.

6. CONCLUSION: WHERE DOES EUROPE GO FROM HERE?

As the foregoing analysis indicates, apart from the Commission's increasingly lonely voice, little positive or forward-looking *European* vision can be detected on immigration and asylum matters. This lack of vision and the inadequacy of the Union's institutional mechanisms have made it extremely difficult to forge consensus on new initiatives and implement them—even when such initiatives amount to little more than the lowest common denominator of the domestic *political* agendas of most member states.[109] Despite ten years of feverish activism, Europe has failed to achieve progress toward harmonization commensurate with the amount of effort and resources expended.

Considering this decade of activism, it is legitimate to ask what returns on its investments Europe has to show. Is the failure to reach harmonization on immigration and asylum policy as relevant to Europe's broader integration effort as this analysis suggests? The answer must be "yes." Europe is engaged in an experiment intended to bring about one of the most fundamental political transformations in recent history. At least one observer has compared what is happening in Europe to the birth-pangs experienced by the United States as it evolved from a confederation to a federation (Nelson 1993). While this analogy is premature, it is useful for drawing attention to both the immensity and *political nature* of

---

[109] It is important not to confuse political agendas with vision. The former are an often narrow and tactical set of decisions geared toward capturing a political advantage. The latter is a set of strategic goals articulated in ways that capture a people's imagination. (Of course, for a vision to be successful it must also outline the practical steps for achieving it.) With few exceptions, the EU fell short of the second criterion on immigration and asylum matters in Delors's early years and proved unequal to both in Delors's last years in office.

the task. (This is a point often overlooked by those who tend to view the exercise through the lens of the technocracy that is so prevalent in Europe's central institutions.) Even if the outcome of this process turns out to be a Union closer to that desired by the United Kingdom (and several of its *sotto voce* allies) than that envisaged by some of Europe's smaller countries and at times Germany (and, until recently, France and Italy), the experiment will have been no less grand or worthwhile—and the challenge no less overwhelming.

WHAT THE RECORD SHOWS

This essay has focused on EC/EU-level policy development on immigration and asylum matters, and on the passionate struggle over "competence" between member states and Europe's central institutions, especially the Commission. In the absence of an overarching vision and an affirmative agenda agreed to by most member states, the discussions have, almost by default, followed two tracks: controls and exclusion on the one hand, and freedom of movement of persons (in the context of the creation of the single market) on the other.

The first track's issues are unquestionably matters of identifiable common interest. On these issues, there has been considerable forward motion, with member states seemingly vetting ideas at the European level to refine their control policies at home. Despite their reluctance to address the various conventions that have been proposed—a rational behavior, given the many reservations about the implications and responsibilities associated with these conventions—all member states have instituted *unilateral* control measures. These range from extensive visa requirements and sanctions on those who transport undocumented individuals to new and streamlined deportation procedures. Most member states have also adopted such restrictions on access to asylum as first- and third-safe country concepts (with or without accompanying bilateral readmission agreements) and accelerated administrative procedures for dispensing with "manifestly unfounded" asylum applications.

The second track focuses on immigration and related matters on which progress is thought to be a prerequisite to attaining the more fundamental aims of the Union—especially on internal freedom of movement, which is the essence of a "single market." On these issues, there has been little real progress. In fact, efforts to promote the integration of third-country nationals (TCNs) have stumbled repeatedly. The European Commission's consistently enlightened, if decreasingly expansive, recommendations have found little resonance among member-state policy makers, who have continued to drag their feet, both within the narrower context of free movement and the much broader context of equal social and economic rights for TCNs. The reasons for this resistance to harmonization include differences over legal interpretation; mistrust of the Commission both for its substantive views and for its perceived arrogance; and genuine political disagreements over the pace, depth, and even desirability of greater policy harmonization on a number of "Justice and Home Affairs" realms. Beyond the reasons for resistance that have been discussed in detail throughout this essay, two additional realities can help us understand developments in their context.

First, in the wake of the Soviet bloc's collapse, Europe was suddenly confronted with a new set of security concerns. The fall of the Berlin Wall led many Western Europeans to worry about the prospect of mass inflows of immigrants and asylum seekers from the East, as well as other threats to internal order stemming from more open borders.[110] These anxieties continued even after it became apparent that, with few exceptions, actual inflows were neither as large nor as consequential as had been predicted. Indeed, anxieties have been *heightened* by fears that harmonization of external border controls would link the success or failure of each country' national controls to those of fourteen others, some of which are thought to lack both the capacity and the political will to control their own borders.

Second, member states are increasingly preoccupied with domestic issues in response to deepening economic uncertainty and perceptions of impending social chaos. When neither Brussels nor national governments appeared able to turn things around, right-wing demagogues were able to rekindle and politically exploit nationalist passions practically overnight—creating deep

---

[110] These include conventional public security issues, such as border and interior controls, and "economic security" matters, including the costs associated with processing large numbers of presumably fraudulent asylum claims and the effects of illegal immigration in undermining labor and tax laws.

crises of legitimacy for ruling parties and reinforcing the voices of those who had argued all along that it is a state's sovereign right and duty to regulate societal membership as a means of preserving social order. This has forced European elites to reexamine the basic premises underlying their support for the Union, and to reconsider the impact of ethnic and cultural diversity on social and political cohesion, thus bringing into question the merits of pursuing a "European" identity.

At the same time, the Community's severe loss of standing with European publics since Maastricht has robbed the European Commission of much of its earlier legitimacy as the "voice" or "conscience" of Europe. The Commission's usually progressive statements on immigration-related matters, systematically support-ed by the European Court and an increasingly engaged European Parliament, kept raising expectations about these institutions' abil-ity to promote the integration of Europe's foreign-born long-term residents and their families.[111] But the record makes clear that these institutions "promised" far greater social, economic, and even political incorporation than was politically possible in most national contexts.

Yet a great deal of policy convergence—most of it heavily weighted in favor of restriction—has in fact taken place in the immigration, refugee, and asylum regimes of member states.[112] *National* policy makers have adopted unilaterally many of the measures that they have been reluctant to adopt collectively. Thus one should not underestimate the degree of deepening intra-EU cooperation that has been achieved. The difficulties of learning to think and act as a single entity on issues on which national politi-cal calculus and perceptions of national interests so often diverge suggest that perhaps no more should be expected from Europe at this time than already has been accomplished.

---

111 Some member states' reluctance, and even outright opposition, to transfering competence over TCNs to the Union is strongly tied to their desire to "evade" judicial scrutiny by the European Court of Justice (see also Schain 1995:12).

112 See Papademetriou and Hamilton 1996 and Papademetriou with Kamali Miyamoto 1996 for a discussion of the immigration and refugee policy regimes of France, Italy, the United Kingdom, and Germany.

THE IMPORTANCE OF TIMING AND CONTEXT

When historians write the definitive account of Europe's quest for integration, the importance of such factors as "timing," "context," and "momentum" (as well as its reverse, "inertia") are likely to be given unusually prominent roles. Timing and context, for instance, were key to Jacques Delors's ability in the mid-1980s to move the Community out of its near-slumber. Delors's genius was his ability to combine the optimism released by dramatic change in Eastern Europe with the sense of confidence born of robust economic growth in Western Europe to provide both impetus and sustenance for the drive to Maastricht.

Context and momentum were equally relevant, however, in undermining Delors's efforts a mere five years later, when the euphoria of the Cold War victory had dissipated, economic prospects were becoming bleak (and unemployment had become Europe's overriding preoccupation), and new crises in the Balkans and the former Soviet Union were fueling popular fears. There was fear that the Community's central institutions not only could not cope but, because of their inability to compel collective actions, might actually be part of the problem. This time, Delors and his Commission failed to appreciate and adapt adequately either to the shifting global dynamic (in which the relative "order" of the Cold War had been replaced by the extraordinary disorder of a myriad local and regional conflicts) or to the domestic political reaction to it. Together, these developments transformed the social and "security" implications of immigration and asylum into intensely contentious matters of "high" politics.

Europe wasted an opportunity to defuse its immigration dilemmas during the prosperous, confident late 1980s, when the political climate was more conducive to enlightened policies. It could have developed comprehensive immigration management strategies and addressed the issues associated with full societal membership for long-term immigrants. When public attitudes soured, national politicians began to search for ways to retreat from intergovernmental cooperation altogether, seeking political comfort instead in rhetoric about sovereign prerogatives and the enactment of national controls and exclusionary measures.

In the current climate, unless the Union manages to recover some of the ground it has lost, any common agenda on immigration and asylum issues will be achieved largely through unilateral

national initiatives or lowest-common-denominator intergovernmental processes. These trends threaten to transform the Union
into a mere discussion forum in which member states can voice
mutual concerns and vet new ideas. While this function is not
insignificant, it falls far short of the Union's promise.

CAN THE UNION AGAIN EXERCISE EFFECTIVE LEADERSHIP?

Few issues are more relevant to the heart and soul of Europe—
or more in need of leadership from the EU—than those associated with asylum and immigration policy. But EU institutions,
especially the Commission, have lost much of their luster and
momentum. There is a nearly universal impression that the EU
bureaucracy—in both its policy-initiation and implementation
functions—is a large part of the problem. Lack of openness and
transparency characterize both process and product.[113] The persis-
tent tendency of European officials to overstate what has been, or
can be, achieved only makes things worse. Typically, it results in
the devaluation of actual achievements and contributes to skepti-
cism about the effectiveness and value of the processes themselves. European institutions can ill-afford such reviews.

Now may be a good time for the Commission to pause and
reflect, even engage in a bit of self-criticism. It should ask itself the
questions suggested throughout this analysis: Why has the Commission failed to provide an *effective* counterweight to the lowest-
common-denominator initiatives advanced by the intergovernmental process? Why has achieving closure on so many key
immigration matters and, to a lesser extent, asylum matters been
so elusive? Are the Commission's priorities and, more fundamen-
tally, its *Weltanschauung*, on many social-policy issues consonant
with those of most EU member states? What effect has the Commission's perceived arrogance had on its ability to inspire the confidence essential to complex working relationships? And finally,
how can the Commission respond to the political and intellectual
shifts away from a "federal" Europe on many of these issues?

---

[113] This is not intended to down-play the need for certain discussions to take place
in a confidential setting. Forcing "sunshine" into idea-generating meetings, for instance, can
have a chilling effect on the discussion, by subjecting governments to public scrutiny for
ideas that may be little more than intellectual exercises and policy musings.

For the Union to be successful on the tough issues, its central institutions (particularly the Commission, but also the Parliament) must develop a clearer appreciation of the concerns and priorities of Europe's publics. They must also show uncharacteristic openness and flexibility, more modesty in their proposals, and far greater sensitivity to the political challenges facing member states. Furthermore, as the Union begins to put together the institutional building blocks for achieving further progress on immigration and related issues, and more generally on issues that arouse strong cultural and social reactions and display even stronger political salience, it will need to think hard about its true priorities, and whether those priorities can best be realized through common, rather than intergovernmental, structures. Central institutions must seek primacy (i.e., competence) only when they can demonstrate that they are better vehicles than member states for achieving a particular end.[114]

Both the EU's central institutions and the Council must reconsider their bureaucratic tendencies and culture of secrecy, which probably have done more to harm Europe's image and to undermine the public's confidence in an affinity with "Europe" than has any single event or decision. European institutions must not be content with incantations about the need to be more accessible. Instead, they must explain how the Union adds measurable value to the life of European "citizens." They must commit to transparency as an end in itself, reaching out to Europeans by explaining what they do, why they do it, and how their actions address and promote important interests. Simultaneously, they must renounce their penchant for the arcane and reexamine, in each instance, whether extreme circumspection, even obfuscation, is necessary or simply a matter of bureaucratic habit. And they absolutely must commit to simplicity and directness in communications. Such terms as "we accept," "we reject," "we have sent back for more study," "we have agreed to 'x' but cannot/will not act on it now because of . . . ." must replace the panoply of obscure and unnecessary "terms of art" that hide what is really being done and what has been accomplished. Ordinary citizens, not just insiders and those trained in interpreting bureaucratic "tea leaves," must be able to understand what is being done, why,

---

114 This is the essence of the principle of *"subsidiarity."* In 1991, EC Commissioner Frans Andriessen (1991:9) defined subsidiarity as meaning "that only those functions which cannot be performed more effectively by local, regional, or national authorities should be transfered to the Community [Union]."

where the process stands, when outcomes can be expected, and precisely how those outcomes will affect their lives. Only then will the extraordinary "democracy" and "relevance" deficits that have plagued the work of Brussels be reduced.

To achieve this, institutional and procedural reforms are needed. Bureaucratic competition between the Commission and the relevant Council Secretariats is probably inevitable, but the awkwardness and inefficiency of the present system suggests that a new and simplified Community structure with effective horizontal relationships is imperative.[115] It is widely recognized that the structures developed during the last Intergovernmental Conference—although they created some order out of the endless ad hoc bodies examining the gamut of Justice and Home Affairs issues—nevertheless had the effect of adding layers to an already cumbersome Community bureaucracy.[116] The 1996 Intergovernmental Conference has a chance to make organizational realignments that will change inter-institution dynamics and improve the chances for moving EU deliberations forward.

Changes in the Commission's management and the need to fully absorb three (and eventually more) new members into the Union—along with the hard rethinking of priorities that the Intergovernmental Conference demands—will dictate a slower pace on immigration and asylum matters, at least for now.[117] This may actually be a blessing in disguise, making it possible for the Commission to recapture lost ground, reconsider its institutional culture, mend fences, focus on the implementation of what already has been agreed,[118] and ultimately create a new image for the

---

[115] Large and complex organizations are organized vertically and hierarchically as much by habit as by default. Yet, in today's complex environment, in which functions frequently cut across portfolios and input from below is as valuable as direction from above, putting together structures in ways that encourage cooperation across competencies in order to achieve policy objectives must receive priority treatment.

[116] In this structure, the Steering Groups must go through the K.4 Committee, which in turn must go through the COREPER, which is responsible for preparing the Council meetings (see figure 5-3, p. 77). Many have complained that the COREPER, composed of generalists responsible for all issue areas, is not as sensitive to immigration matters as it perhaps ought to be.

[117] The frenetic pace of work in these areas has had two unanticipated consequences. The first is a widespread sense of "fatigue," that in turn affects the quality of decision-making. The second, related consequence is that key participants begin to confuse the kinetic energy surrounding "process" with progress.

[118] This is an issue of immense long-term consequences yet one that has received scant attention by analysts. EU observers have long been concerned about the slow pace of

Unions's central institutions. Misgivings by several member states about the Commission's policy judgment, and reactions to its political instincts that range from puzzlement to contempt, have periodically isolated the Commission in discussions where its input and expertise should have been welcome and would have been useful. If the Commission comes to be seen as a cooperative, pragmatic, responsible, and accountable body whose ideas, program initiatives, and management style deserve respect, both its fortunes and the cause of Europe stand a good chance to advance.

Perhaps the Commission might find a new and constructive role for itself as a kind of "think tank," helping to inform and act as a catalyst for rather than dominate the process of finding a collective voice on immigration and asylum matters. In taking up such a role, the Commission might usefully focus on four principal areas:

(1) Continuing to make progress on the issues of understanding better and seeking to affect the root causes of emigration, establishing effective border controls, and initially coordinating and eventually harmonizing asylum and immigration policies;

(2) Achieving greater harmony between on-the-ground reality and policy responses on immigration and asylum matters, partly through the establishment of the proposed immigration "observatory";

(3) Continuing pursuit of the TCN integration agenda; and,

(4) Developing a better model for European-wide management and funding of refugee emergencies.

It is important to remember, however, that trial and error is inevitable when sensitive socio-cultural, policy, and law-and-order issues like those related to immigration and asylum flows are at stake. Regardless of Europe's eventual shape, the timetable of "coming together" will be much longer than even the most clairvoyant observers now estimate, and policy evolution will necessarily be complex, perhaps even unpredictable. Appreciating these truths about the enterprise is essential to understanding not only its ebbs and flows, but also the many inevitable instances when the process will appear to have ground to a halt.

---

implementing agreed-upon matters, especially the continuing barriers to even the commercial elements of the single market. Members states' dragging their feet in adjusting their national legislation to Community/Union rules has long been the "dirty little secret" of Europe's drive toward integration.

REFERENCES

Ad Hoc Group on Immigration (AHIG). 1990. "Draft Convention determining the State responsible for examining applications for asylum lodged in one of the Member States of the European Communities." June 12. (SN 2492/2/90 WGI 623 AS87.) Brussels.

——. 1991a. "Summary of conclusions of the meetings of the Ministers concerned with immigration held in London (20 October 1986), Brussels (28 April 1987), Athens (9 December 1988), Madrid (12 May 1989), Paris (15 December 1989), Dublin (15 June 1990), and Rome (7 December 1990)." February 7. (SN 1131/91 WGI 735.) Brussels.

——. 1991b. "Convention between the Member States of the European Community on the crossing of their external frontiers." May. (SN 2535/91 WGI 829.) Brussels.

——. 1991c. "Report from the Ministers Responsible for Immigration to the European Council Meeting in Maastricht on Immigration and Asylum Policy." December 3. (SN 4038/91 WGI 930.) Brussels.

——. 1991d. "Summary of Conclusions of the Subgroup on Asylum." December 20. (SN 4374/91 WGI 939 AS 101). Brussels.

——. 1992a. "Implementation of the Convention determining the State responsible for examination applications for asylum lodged in one of the Members States of the European Communities." March 18. (SN 1903/92 WGI 1028 AS 115.) Brussels.

——. 1992b. "Preliminary draft Convention 'parallel' to the Dublin Convention of 15 June 1990." May 8. (SN 1729/2/92 WGI 1008 REV 2.) Brussels.

——. 1992c. "Definition and Harmonized Application of the Principle of the First Host Country - Draft Conclusions." May 21. (SN 2520/92 WGI 1102.) Brussels.

——. 1992d. "Draft Conclusions on the implementation of controls on persons under the Convention on the crossing of external frontiers." May 21. (SN 2782/1/92 WGI 1108 REV 1.) Brussels.

——. 1992e. "Harmonization of national policies on admission for employment - Draft resolution for adoption by Immigration Ministers of Members States of the EC meeting inter-governmentally on 30 November/1 December 1992." July 24. (SN 2611/92 WGI 1165.) Brussels.

——. 1992f. "Note by the U.K. Presidency: Draft resolution for adoption by EC Immigration Ministers (and Employment) Ministers." October 22. (SN 4286/92 WGI 1234.) Brussels.

——. 1992g. "Countries in which there is generally no serious risk of persecution." November 18. (SN 4821/92 WGI 1281 AS 145.) Brussels.

————. 1992h. "Draft Resolution on a harmonized approach to questions concerning host third countries." November 19. (SN 4823/92 WGI 1283 AS 14.) Brussels.

————. 1992i. "Resolution on manifestly unfounded applications for asylum." December 2. (SN 4822/1/92 REV 1 WGI 1282 AS 146.) Brussels.

————. 1992j. "Draft conclusions of the meeting of Ministers with responsibility for immigration (London, 30 November to 1 December 1992)." December 2. (SN 4824/1/92 WGI 1284 REV 1.) Brussels.

————. 1992k. "Work programme for the ad hoc Group on Immigration under the Danish Presidency (first half of 1993)." December 15. (SN 5109/92 WGI 1300.) Brussels.

————. 1993a. "Compilation of texts on European practice with respect to asylum" May 14. (SN 2836/93 WGI 1505.) Brussels.

————. 1993b. "Resolution on certain common guidelines as regards the admission of particularly vulnerable groups from the former Yugoslavia." May 14. (SN 2830/93 WGI 1499.) Brussels.

————. 1993c. "First Activity Report from CIREA to the Ministers Responsible for Immigration." May 14. (SN 2834/93 WGI 1503 CIREA 66.) Brussels.

————. 1993d. "Draft Recommendation concerning checks on and expulsion of third country nationals residing or working without authorization (adopted by the Ministers Responsible for Immigration at their meeting on 1 - 2 June 1993 in Copenhagen)." May 25. (SN 3017/93 WGI 1516.) Brussels.

————. 1993e. "Harmonization of National Policies on Family Reunification." June 3. (SN 2828/1/93 WGI 1497 REV 1.) Brussels.

————. 1993f. "Report on the completion of the Maastricht programme on asylum adopted in 1991." October 19. (SN 4512/1/93 WGI 1654 REV 1.) Brussels.

Andriessen, Frans H. J. J. 1991. "The Integration of Europe: It's Now or Never," in *European Affairs,* Number 6 (December):6-11.

Borchardt, Klaus-Dieter. 1994. *The ABC of Community Law.* October 1993. Luxembourg: Office for Official Publications of the European Communities.

————. 1995. *European Integration: The Origins and Growth of the European Community.* January 15. Luxembourg: Office for Official Publications of the European Communities.

Bourdouvalis, Chris. 1994. "The European Union and its Quest for a Common Immigration Policy: Problems and Possible Solutions." Draft paper prepared for the European Community Studies Association Meeting, Charleston, South Carolina, 13-14 May 1994.

Bunyan, Tony, and Frances Webber. 1995. *Intergovernmental Cooperation on Immigration and Asylum.* Briefing Paper No. 19 (April). Brussels: Churches Commission for Migrants in Europe (CCME).

Callovi, Giuseppe. 1990. "Regulating Immigration in the European Community: Effects of the Single European Act upon migration policies and on the decision making process in this area." Lecture to an International Conference of Europeanists sponsored by the Council for European Studies, Washington, D.C., 23-25 March 1990.

————. 1992. "Regulation of Immigration in 1993: Pieces of the European Community Jig-Saw Puzzle," *International Migration Review.* Vol. 26, No. 2. (Summer), 353-372. New York: Center for Migration Studies.

————. 1995. Private Interview. June 29. Washington, D.C.

Center for Information, Discussion and Exchange on Asylum (CIREA). 1993. "Second activity report on CIREA—Version for Publication." December 22. (10043/1/93 REV 1 CIREA 9.) Brussels.

Christian Science Monitor. 1995. Ben Jones. "Immigration Pushes Europe to Steady Southern Fringe." November 24:6.

Coleman, D.A. "Europe Under Migration Pressure: Some Facts On Immigration." Draft paper presented at the European Community Studies Association Workshop on Immigration into Western Societies: Implications and Policy Choices, May 13-14, 1994, Charleston, South Carolina.

Collinson, Sarah. 1994. *Beyond Borders: West European Migration Policy Towards the 21st Century.* Washington, D.C.: Brookings Institution.

Commission of the European Communities. 1985a. "Guidelines for a Community Policy on Migration." Commission communication transmitted to the Council on 7 March 1985 (COM [85] 48 final). As printed in the Bulletin of the European Communities, Supplement 9/85. Luxembourg: Office for Official Publications of the European Communities.

————. 1985b. "Commission Decision of 8 July 1985 setting up a prior communication and consultation procedure on migration policies in relation to non-member countries." As reproduced in the Bulletin of the European Communities, Supplement 9/85. Luxembourg: Office for Official Publications of the European Communities.

————. 1988. "Completing the Internal Market: An Area without Internal Frontiers. The Progress Report Required by Article 8b of the Treaty." November 17. (COM[88]650 final). Brussels.

————. 1989. "The social integration of third-country migrants residing on a permanent and lawful basis in the Member States." June 22. (SEC[89] 924 final.) Brussels.

————. 1990a. "Community Charter of the Fundamental Social Rights of Workers." (adopted December 9, 1989). Luxembourg: Office for Official Publications of the European Communities.

————. 1990b. "Policies on Immigration and the Social Integration of Migrants in the European Community." Expert's Report drawn up on behalf of the Commission of the European Communities. September 28. (SEC[90]1813.) Brussels.

————. 1990c. "Completing the Internal Market: An Area without Internal Frontiers. Progress Report Required by Article 8b of the Treaty." November 23. (COM[90]552 final). Brussels.

————. 1991a. "Population Trends and Europe (mandate of 21 June 1989)." (Commission Staff working paper.) April 19. (SEC[91]766). Brussels.

————. 1991b. "Communication from the Commission to the Council and the European Parliament on the right of asylum." October 11. (SEC[91]1857 final.) Brussels.

————. 1991c. "Communication to the Council and the European Parliament on Immigration." October 23. (SEC[91]1855 final.) Brussels.

————. 1992a. "From the Single European Act to Maastricht and Beyond. The Means to Match our Ambitions." February 11. (COM[92]2000 final). Brussels.

————. 1992b. "Abolition of Border Controls. Commission Communication to the Council and to Parliament." May 8. (SEC[92]877 final.) Brussels.

————. 1992c. "Family reunification in the light of international law, Community law and Member States' laws and/or practices." (Commission staff working document.) May 13. (V/384/92). Brussels.

————. 1992d. "Immigration Policies in the Member States: Between the Need for Control and the Desire for Integration." (Working document.) Summary report of the information network in migration from non EC countries (RIMET in its French acronym). May. (V/1020/92.) Brussels.

————. 1992e. "Creation of CIREFI. Commission Information Sources on migration" (Commission staff working paper.) November 16. (SEC[92]2167). Brussels.

————. 1993a. "Legal Instruments to Combat Racism and Xenophobia. Comparative assessment of the legal instruments implemented in the various Member States to combat all forms of discrimination, racism and xenophobia and incitement to hatred and racial violence." December 1992. Luxembourg: Office for Official Publications of the European Communities.

————. 1993b. "Report to the Council on the possibility of applying Article K.9 of the Treaty on European Union to asylum policy." November 4. (SEC[93]1687 final.) Brussels.

————. 1993c. "Communication to the Council and the European Parliament. (I) Proposal for a Decision, based on Article K.3. of the Treaty on European Union, establishing the Convention on the crossing of external frontiers of the Member States; (II) Proposal for a regulation based on Article 100c of the Treaty establishing the European Communities, determining the third countries whose nationals must be in possession of a visa when crossing the external borders of the Member States." December 10. (COM[93]684 final.) Brussels.

————. 1994a. "Communication from the Commission to the Council and the European Parliament on Immigration and Asylum Policies." February 23. (COM[94]23 final). Brussels.

————. 1994b. "Proposal for a Council Directive laying down detailed arrangements for the exercise of the right to vote and to stand as a candidate in municipal elections by citizens of the Union residing in a Member State of which they are not nationals." February 23. (COM[94]38 final.) Brussels.

————. 1994c. "The Community Internal Market. 1993 Report." March 14. COM[94]55 final). Brussels.

————. 1994d. "Communication from the Commission to the Council of the European Parliament on a European Union action plan to combat drugs - 1995-1999." June 23. (COM[94]234 final). Brussels.

————. 1994e. "Mission Report on the Vouliagmeni Conference on Immigration and the European Union: Building on a comprehensive approach." June 26-28. Brussels.

————. 1994f. "European Social Policy—A Way Forward for the Union. A White Paper." July 27. (COM[94]333.) Brussels.

————. 1995. "Medium Term Social Action Programme 1995-1997." April 12. (COM[95]134 final.) Brussels.

Committee of Permanent Representatives (COREPER). 1993a. "Guidelines for joint reports on third countries. June 3. (7471/94 CIREA 16.) Brussels.

————. 1993b. "Implementation of the Dublin Convention - Means of proof." November 19. (10300/93 ASIM 19.) Brussels.

————. 1993c. "Draft Council conclusions concerning the possible application of Article K.9 of the Treaty on European Union to asylum policy." November 25. (10360/93 ADD 1 ASIM 21.) Brussels.

————. 1993d. "Draft Council conclusions concerning the possible application of Article K.9 of the Treaty on European Union to asylum policy." November 26. (10360/93 ASIM 21.) Brussels.

————. 1994a. "Draft Council conclusions concerning the possible application of Article K.9 of the Treaty on European Union to asylum policy." June 3. (7468/94 ASIM 110.) Brussels.

————. 1994b. "Implementation of the Dublin Convention - Transfer of asylum applicant." June 3. (7470/94 ASIM 112). Brussels.

————. 1994c. "Procedure for drawing up reports in connection with joint assessments of the situation from third countries." June 3. (7472/94 CIREA 17.) Brussels.

————. 1994d. "CIREA - Circulation and confidentiality of joint reports on the situation in certain third countries." June 3. (7473/94 CIREA 18.) Brussels.

————. 1994e. "Second activity report on CIREA." June 3. (7474/94 CIREA 19.) Brussels.

————. 1994f. "Resolution on limitations on admissions of third country nationals to the Member States for employment." June 20. (7760/94 [Presse 128-G].) Brussels.

————. 1994g. "Minimum guarantees for asylum procedures." November 23. (11217/94 JAI 61.) Brussels.

————. 1994h. "Draft Council Resolution on the admission of third country nationals to the territory of the Members States of the European Union for study purposes." November 24. (11218/94 JAI 62.) Brussels.

————. 1995. "Draft Resolution on minimum guarantees for asylum procedures." March 2. (5354/96.) Brussels.

Coordinators' Group on Free Movement of Persons. 1989. "Free Movement of Persons. Report to the European Council by the Coordinators' Group (Palma Document)." Report drawn up at its June 5-6 meeting in Palma de Mallorca, Spain. June 9. (CIRC 3624/89.)

————. 1990a. Report from the Coordinators' Group on the Free Movement of Persons to the European Council." June 17. (CIRC 3627/1/90.) Brussels.

————. 1990b. "Inventory on Migration." November 7. (CIRC 3645/1/90 REV. 1.) Brussels.

————. 1991a. "Report to the Luxembourg European Council from the Chairman of the Coordinators' Group on Free Movement of Persons." June 24. (CIRC 3640/91). Brussels.

————. 1991b. "Report to the European Council from the Chairman of the Coordinators' Group on Free Movement of Persons - Work done during first half of 1991." June 24-26. (CIRC 3640/91 ADD 1 REV 1.) Brussels.

————. 1991c. "Report to the European Council in Maastricht from the Coordinators' Group on Free Movement of Persons." December 5. (CIRC 3677/91.) Brussels.

————. 1992a. "Implementation of the Treaty on European Union in the fields of justice and home affairs. Report from the Coordinators on the Free Movement of Persons to the Personal Representatives." April 29. (CIRC 3624/2/92 REV.2.) Brussels.

————. 1992b. "Implementation of the Treaty on European Union in the fields of justice and home affairs." June 17. (CIRC 3624/2/92 REV. 2 ADD 1.) Brussels.

————. 1992c. "Report to the European Council in Lisbon from the Coordinators on Free Movement of Persons (prev. doc. CIRC 3643/92)." June 19. (CIRC 3647/92.) Brussels.

————. 1992d. "Progress made in implementing the Palma Report." November 5. (CIRC 3658/4/92 REV. 4.) Brussels.

————. 1992e. "Report to the European Council in Edinburgh from the Coordinators' Group on Free Movement of Persons." November 23. (CIRC 3687/92.) Brussels.

Council of Ministers of the European Communities/Union (Council). 1991. "Non-Paper—Draft Treaty Articles with a View to Achieving Political Union." April 12. As published in *Europe, Agence Internationale d'Information pour la Presse*. No. 1709/1710 (May 3). Brussels.

————. 1992a. "Common Position Adopted by the Council on 30 April 1992 with a View to Adopting a Regulation Amending Part II of Regulation (EEC) No. 1612/68 on Freedom of Movement for Workers Within the Community." April 30. (5253/1/92 REV 1 SOC 100 PRO-COOP 19.) Brussels.

————. 1992b. "Results of the Meeting of Ministers responsible for Immigration (London, 30 November - 1 December 1992)." December 2. (10579/92 IMMIG 2.) Brussels.

————. 1993. "Press Release - Meeting of Ministers with responsibility for immigration (Copenhagen, 1 and 2 June 1993)." June 2. Brussels.

————. 1994a. "Harmonized application of the definition of refugee status in Article 1 of the Geneva Convention." March 31. (4245/2/95 REV 2 ASIM 8.) Brussels.

————. 1994b. "Information Exchange Agreement between CDR/[UN]HCR and CIREA." May 16. (6958/94 CIREA 13.) Brussels.

————. 1994c. "Work programme for Steering Group I for the second half of 1994." June 14. (7735/94 ASIM 120.) Brussels.

————. 1994d. "Work programme of CIREA for the second half of 1994." June 15. (7846/94 CIREA 20.) Brussels.

————. 1994e. "Draft Council Resolution on the admission of third-country nationals to the territory of the Members States of the European Union for study purposes." June 22. (7996/94 ASIM 127.) Brussels.

————. 1994f. "Concentration and Cooperation on the Implementation of Repatriation Measures." July 12. (8410/94 ASIM 140; translated from German.) Brussels.

————. 1994g. "Draft conclusions on the taking back by Member States of persons who are illegally resident in the territory of a Member State, but who hold a residence permit of another Member State." July 22. (8557/94 ASIM 149.) Brussels.

————. 1994h. "Minimum Guarantees for Asylum Proceedings." July 25. (8713/94 ASIM 152; translated from German.) Brussels.

————. 1994i. "Burden sharing with regard to the admission and residence on a temporary basis of displaced persons; state of discussions." November 17. (10881/94 JAI 47.) Brussels.

————. 1994j. "Council Decision on a joint action adopted by the Council on the basis of Article K.3 2(b) of the Treaty on European Union concerning travel facilities for school pupils from third countries resident in a Member State." November 21. (10902/94 JAI 51, as corrected November 25.) Brussels.

————. 1994k. "Draft Resolution on minimum guarantees for asylum procedures." December 7. (11217/94 ADD 1 JAI 61.) Brussels.

————. 1994l. "Resolution relating to limitations on the admission of third country nationals to the territory of the Member States for the purpose of pursuing activities as self-employed persons." Adopted November 30-December 1. (11219/94). Brussels.

Council of Europe (COE). 1991a. "Conference of Ministers on the Movement of Persons from Central and Eastern European Countries" held in Vienna, January 24-25. Final Communique (MMP [91] 7.)

————. 1991b. "Fourth Conference of European Ministers Responsible for Migration Affairs" held in Luxembourg, September 17-18. Conclusions and Resolution adopted by the Conference (MMG-4 [91] 9 final.)

————. 1993. "Conference to Prevent Uncontrolled Migration" held in Budapest, February 15-16. Draft Recommendations.

Cruz, Antonio. 1993. *Schengen, ad hoc Immigration Group, and other European Intergovernmental Bodies in view of a Europe without Internal Borders.* Briefing Paper No. 12 (June). Brussels: Churches Committee for Migrants in Europe (CCME).

de Jong, C. Dennis. 1994. "European Immigration Policies in the 21st Century." Paper presented at the European Community Studies Association Workshop, *Immigration into Western Societies: Implications and Policy Choices.* May 13-14. Charleston, South Carolina.

————. 1995. Private Interview. July 3. Washington, D.C.

The Economist. 1995a. "France prepares for EMU." December 9:11-12.

————. 1995b. "The Challenge to EMU." December 9:19-21.

————. 1995c. "The strength in Juppe's inability to yield." December 9:49-50.

————. 1995d. "European Union: In battle order." December 9:53.

Eucarer, Emek. M. 1995. "Europe's Search for Policy: Asylum Policy Harmonization and European Integration." Draft paper presented at the European Community Studies Association Conference, May 13-14, Charleston, South Carolina.

The European. 1995a. Anne-Elisabeth Moutet and Victor Smart. "Desperate Kohl offers Chirac his hotline promises." December 7-13:1

————. 1995b. Editorial. "A serious misjudgment." December 7-13:10.

————. 1995c. Klaus Engelen. "It's make or break for Paris and Bonn." December 7-13:18.

European Commission Delegation to the United States. 1994. *The European Union: A Guide.* Washington, D.C.: European Commission Delegation to the United States.

————. 1996. *Serving the European Union: A Citizen's Guide to the Institutions of the European Union.*

European Communities. 1987. *Treaties establishing the European Communities (ECSC, EEC, EAEC); Single European Act; Other basic instruments (Abridged Edition).* Luxembourg: Office for Official Publications of the European Community.

————. 1990. *Convention Determining the State Responsible for Examining Applications for Asylum Lodged in One of the Member States of the European Communities.* Signed June 15 in Dublin, Ireland. (CONV/ASILE).

————. 1992. *Treaty on European Union.* Luxembourg: Office for Official Publications of the European Communities.

European Council. 1986a. "European Council in The Hague. Conclusions of the Presidency." June 26-27. As printed in *Bulletin of the European Communities - Commission,* Vol. 19, No. 6-1986. Luxembourg: Office for Official Publications of the European Communities.

————. 1986b. "European Council in London. Conclusions of the Presidency." December 6. As printed in *Bulletin of the European Communities - Commission.* Vol. 19, No. 12-1986. Luxembourg: Office for Official Publications of the European Communities.

————. 1988. "European Council in Hanover. Conclusions of the Presidency." June 27-28. As printed in *Bulletin of the European Communities - Commission.* Vol. 21, No. 6-1988. Luxembourg: Office for Official Publications of the European Communities.

————. 1989. "European Council in Strasbourg. Conclusions of the Presidency." December 8-9. As printed in *Bulletin of the European Communities - Commission.* Vol. 22, No. 12-1989. Luxembourg: Office for Official Publications of the European Communities.

————. 1992. "European Council in Edinburgh. Conclusions of the Presidency." December 11-12. As printed in *The European Council: Conclusions of the Presidency 1992-1994*. Brussels: European Commission, Directorate-General for Information, Communication, Culture, and Audiovisual (1995).

————. 1993. "European Council in Brussels. Conclusions of the Presidency." December 10-11. As printed in *The European Council: Conclusions of the Presidency 1992-1994*. Brussels: European Commission, Directorate-General for Information, Communication, Culture, and Audiovisual (1995).

————. 1994a. "European Council in Corfu. Conclusions of the Presidency." June 24-25. As printed in *The European Council: Conclusions of the Presidency 1992-1994*. Brussels: European Commission, Directorate-General for Information, Communication, Culture, and Audiovisual (1995).

————. 1994b. "European Council in Essen. Conclusions of the Presidency." December 9-10. As printed in *The European Council: Conclusions of the Presidency 1992-1994*. Brussels: European Commission, Directorate-General for Information, Communication, Culture, and Audiovisual (1995).

European Court of Justice (ECJ). 1977. *Regina v. Pierre Bouchereau* ("Public Policy") (Preliminary Ruling requested by the Marlborough Street Magistrates' Court, London). Judgment of the Court of 27 October. As printed in *European Court Reports*, 30/77 ECR 1535-2029. Luxembourg: Office of the Official Publications of the European Communities.

————. 1987. "Judgment of the Court in Joined Cases 281, 283 to 285 and 287/85 (Germany, France, Netherlands, Denmark, and the United Kingdom v. Commission) on Application for the annulment of Commission Decision 85/381/EEC of 8 July 1985 setting up a prior communication and consultation procedure on migration policies in relation to non-member countries." July 9. As published in *European Court Reports*, [1987] ECR 2919-3452. Luxembourg: Office of the Official Publications of the European Communities.

European Ministers of the Interior. 1994. "Conclusions du President de la Reunion Informelle des Ministres des Affaires Interieures Reunis a Thessaloniki." May 6. Brussels.

European Parliament (EP). 1993. "Report of the Committee on Civil Liberties and Internal Affairs on the resurgence of racism and xenophobia in Europe and the danger of right wing extremist violence." April 1. (A3-0127/93; DOC EN2525100). Luxembourg.

Financial Times. 1995a. Judy Dempsey and Michael Lindemann. "Germany's CDU calls for EU majority voting." June 14:2.

————. 1995b. Editorial. "Kohl treads carefully." June 14:15.

————. 1995c. Emma Tucker and Hugh Carnegy. "Nordic nations seek to join EU Schengen area." October 9:22.

————. 1995d. Emma Tucker. "Schengen pact open to non-EU members." October 25:3.

————. 1995e. Lionel Barber. "Brussels keeps shut the gates to the east." November 16:17.

————. 1995f. Emma Tucker. "EU criticised over new refugee policy." November 24:2.

————. 1995g. Tom Burns. "EU turns attention to southern flank." November 27:4.

————. 1995h. Emma Tucker. "Racism row set to haunt Madrid summit." December 13:2.

————. 1995i. Lionel Barber. "Union struggles to regain its sense of direction." December 15:2.

————. 1995j. Caroline Southey. "Compromise on expansion." December 18:2.

Guild, Elspeth. 1992. *Protecting migrants' rights: application of EC agreements with third countries.* Briefing Paper No. 10 (November). Brussels: CCME.

Hix, Simon. 1995. *The 1996 Intergovernmental conference and the future of the third pillar.* Briefing Paper No. 20 (June). Brussels: CCME.

International Herald Tribune. 1995. Tom Buerkle. "EU's Internal Disputes Stall Membership Drive in East." December 12:5.

Justice and Home Affairs (JHA/JAI) Council. 1993a. "1710th Council Meeting—Justice and Home Affairs." November 29-30. (10550/93 [Presse 209].) Brussels.

————. 1993b. "Priority work programme for 1994 and structures to be set up in the field of Justice and Home Affairs." December 2. (10684/93 JAI 12.) Brussels.

————. 1994a "1738th Council Meeting - Justice and Home Affairs." March 23. (5760/94 [Presse 45].) Brussels.

————. 1994b. "Draft Minutes of the 1738th Council meeting (Justice and Home Affairs)." April 6. (5806/94 PV/CONS 11 JAI 7, as subsequently corrected [COR 1 REV 1] on May 27.) Brussels.

————. 1994c. "1771st Council Meeting - Justice and Home Affairs." June 20. (7760/94 [Presse 128-G].) Luxembourg.

————. 1994d. "Implementation of the Action Plan in the field of Justice and Home Affairs." November 24. (11347/94 JAI 67.) Brussels.

————. 1995a. "Draft Resolution on burden-sharing with regard to the admission and residence of displaced persons on a temporary basis." March 17. (5832/95 ASIM 91.) Brussels.

————. 1995b. "1885th Council Meeting - Justice and Home Affairs." November 23. (11720/95 [Presse 332].) Brussels.

K.4 Committee. 1994a. "Commission communication on immigration and asylum policies–Draft Council conclusions. June 2. (7465/94 JAI 14; previous 5187/94 ASIM 49.) Brussels.

————. 1994b. "Standard travel document for the removal/expulsion of third country foreign nationals–Draft Council Recommendation." November 9. (10721/94 JAI 43.) Brussels.

————. 1994c. "Draft Council conclusions on the organisation and development of the Centre for Information, Discussion and Exchange on the crossing of frontiers and immigration (CIREFI)." November 14. (10884/94 JAI 50.) Brussels.

K.4 Committee, Steering Group I (Asylum/Immigration) (SGI). 1994a. "Implementation of the Dublin Convention–Transfer of an asylum applicant." November 8 and 9. (9950/93 ASIM 7.) Brussels.

————. 1994b. "Second activity report on CIREA." November 15. (9940/93 CIREA 5.) Brussels.

Migration News Sheet. 1995a . "Convention on Checks at the External Borders." No. 142/95-01 (January):1. Brussels: European Information Network (EIN).

————. 1995b. "Commission Strongly Criticizes Functioning of Third Pilllar." No. 147/95-06 (June):1. Brussels: European Information Network (EIN).

————. 1995c. "Despite Optimistic Declarations, France Mistrusts Checks Carried out at Certain External Borders." No. 147/95-06 (June):2. Brussels: EIN.

————. 1995d. "Treaty Must be Revised to Include Community Competence to Combat Racism." No. 147/95-06 (June):8. Brussels: EIN.

————. 1995e. "Europol - Opt-out Clause for U.K." No. 147/95-07 (July):1. Brussels: EIN.

————. 1995f. "France Still Hesitates to Apply [Schengen] Convention." No. 147/95-07 (July):2-3. Brussels: EIN.

————. 1995g. "The 15 Adopt Principles of Sharing out the Costs of Temporary Reception of Displaced Persons." No. 147/95-07 (July):5. Brussels: EIN.

Monnet, Jean. 1978. *Memoires (with an introduction by George W. Ball)*. Garden City, N.Y.: Doubleday. (Translated from the French by Richard Mayne).

Muus, Philip J. 1994.   Letter to Commission staff member Dennis de Jong regarding Research on aspects of root causes of international migration. June 7 (Brussels). Copy on file at the Carnegie Endowment for International Peace.

Niessen, Jan. 1992. "European Community Legislation and Intergovernmental Cooperation on Migration," in *International Migration Review*, Vol. 26, No. 2 (Summer), 676-684. New York: Center for Migration Studies.

————. 1995. Interview. January 25. Washington, D.C.

Papademetriou, Demetrios G. 1993. "Confronting the Challenge of Transnational Migration: Domestic and International Responses" in *The Changing Course of International Migration.* Paris: Organisation for Economic Co-Operation and Development (OECD).

Papademetriou, Demetrios G., and Kimberly Hamilton. 1995. *Managing Uncertainty: Regulating Immigration Flows in Advanced Industrial Countries.* Washington, D.C.: Carnegie Endowment for International Peace.

————. 1996. *Converging Paths to Restriction: French, Italian, and British Responses to Immigration.* Washington, D.C.: Carnegie Endowment for International Peace.

Papademetriou, Demetrios G., with Maryam Kamali Miyamoto. 1996 (forthcoming). *Germany's Wavering Welcome to Newcomers* (working title). Washington, D.C.: Carnegie Endowment for International Peace.

Schain, Martin A. 1995. "Policy Effectiveness and the Regulation of Immigration in Europe." Paper presented at the Annual Meeting of the International Studies Association, Chicago, IL. February 25.

Trevi Group. 1990. "Meeting of Ministers of Justice and of the Interior of the European Community: Press Communique." June 14-15. Dublin.

U.S. Commission for the Study of International Migration and Cooperative Economic Development. 1990. *Unauthorized Migration: An Economic Development Response.* Washington, D.C.: U.S. Commission for the Study of International Migration and Cooperative Economic Development (July).

Wall Street Journal Classroom Edition. 1992. Mark M. Nelson. "Europe's Struggle Reflected in a Distant American Mirror." November:20.

Washington Post. 1995. William Drozdiak. "Europe Views Euro as Savior of Union." December 17:32.

Vos, Hans. 1995. "Letter to Demetrios G. Papademetriou." April 18. (On file at the Carnegie Endowment for International Peace.) Washington, D.C.

ACKNOWLEDGMENTS

This study is the fifth in the series on international migration and refugee policy issues published by the International Migration Policy Program of the Carnegie Endowment for International Peace. Together wih *Converging Paths to Restriction: French, Italian, and British Responses to Migration* and the forthcoming *A Study in Ambiguity: Germany's Wavering Welcome to Newcomers*, it forms a trilogy that critiques Western Europe's responses to migration on the eve of the 21st century.

The migration issue has become too complex to address effectively without relying extensively on the written and unwritten perspectives and ideas of others—more so than even the most complete footnotes and bibliographies can hope to document. I would therefore like to acknowledge an intellectual debt to my colleagues in the many meetings held under the auspices of the Organisation for Economic Co-operation and Development (OECD): the OECD's Migration Working Party, on which I have served since 1988 and which I have had the privilege to chair since 1992; the technical experts' discussions associated with the Continuous Reporting System on Migration (better known by its French acronym, SOPEMI) on which I served from 1988 to 1992 and which I continue to attend whenever an opportunity arises; and the three hugely successful conferences on these issues (in Rome in 1991, Madrid in 1994, and Tokyo in 1995). All have proven to be extraordinary educational opportunities.

Extensive formal and informal conversations with senior European Community officials and analysts on these issues over the years have served a similar role. I have had access to numerous official documents, many of them confidential, with which to reconstruct the development of Community policy on immigration and asylum. Given this unusual opportunity, I have attempted to create as complete a record as possible, while reserving the privileges of analysis and commentary.

I would like to thank Giuseppe Callovi, Jean-Pierre Garson, C. Dennis de Jong, and Hans Vos for their painstaking and detailed critique of the manuscript and for their encouragement for the project. Because of the complexity of the issues it addresses, this book has required much deeper commitments from its pre-publication readers/critics than is customary. I would particularly like to acknowledge with extreme gratitude the assistance of Lori Lindburg, who acted both as a research assistant and editor, but who also repeatedly updated the work as publication target dates kept slipping; her thoughtfulness has vastly improved the manuscript. As was true of the earlier volumes in the series, Yasmin Santiago deserves special mention, not only for guiding and managing the manuscript from its inception to its publication, but also for her patient research assistance during the project's early stages. At that time, she waded through the various versions of official papers with good humor, trying to make early sense out of the maze of community verbiage. For this I am most grateful.

Finally, I would also like to give credit and thanks to Patricia W. Blair and Rosemarie Philips for their editorial contributions. As is both proper and customary to acknowledge, any errors of commission or omission rest squarely with the author.

Demetrios G. Papademetriou

ABOUT THE AUTHOR

DEMETRIOS G. PAPADEMETRIOU

Mr. Papademetriou is a Senior Associate of the Carnegie Endowment for International Peace and directs its International Migration Policy Program. He also serves as Chair of the OECD Migration Committee. His work concentrates on evaluating the adequacy of U.S. immigration policies and practices in meeting U.S. interests; the migration politics and policies of European and other advanced industrial societies; and the role of multilateral institutions in developing and coordinating collective responses to international population movements.

Mr. Papademetriou has published extensively in the United States and abroad on the immigration and refugee policies of the United States and other advanced industrial societies, the impact of legal and illegal immigration on the U.S. labor market, and the relationship between international migration and development. Prior to joining the Endowment, Mr. Papademetriou served as Director of Immigration Policy and Research at the U.S. Department of Labor and chaired the Secretary of Labor's Immigration Policy Task Force. Mr. Papademetriou has also served as Executive Editor of the International Migration Review. He has taught at American University, Duke University, the University of Maryland, and the Graduate Faculty of the New School of Social Research.

THE CARNEGIE ENDOWMENT FOR INTERNATIONAL PEACE

The Carnegie Endowment for International Peace was established in 1910 in Washington, D.C., with a gift from Andrew Carnegie. As a tax-exempt operating (not grant-making) foundation, the Endowment conducts programs of research, discussion, publication, and education in international affairs and U.S. foreign policy. The Endowment publishes the quarterly magazine, *Foreign Policy*.

Carnegie's senior associates—whose backgrounds include government, journalism, law, academia, and public affairs—bring to their work substantial first-hand experience in foreign policy through writing, public and media appearances, study groups, and conferences. Carnegie associates seek to invigorate and extend both expert and public discussion on a wide range of international issues, including worldwide migration, nuclear nonproliferation, regional conflicts, multilateralism, democracy-building, and the use of force. The Endowment also engages in and encourages projects designed to foster innovative contributions in international affairs.

In 1993, the Carnegie Endowment committed its resources to the establishment of a public policy research center in Moscow designed to promote intellectual collaboration among scholars and specialists in the United States, Russia, and other post-Soviet states. Together with the Endowment's associates in Washington, the center's staff of Russian and American specialists conduct programs on a broad range of major policy issues ranging from economic reform to civil-military relations. The Carnegie Moscow Center holds seminars, workshops, and study groups at which international participants from academia, government, journalism, the private sector, and nongovernmental institutions gather to exchange views. It also provides a forum for prominent international figures to present their views to informed Moscow audiences. Associates of the center also host seminars in Kiev on an equally broad set of topics.

The Endowment normally does not take institutional positions on public policy issues. It supports its activities principally from its own resources, supplemented by nongovernmental, philanthropic grants.

THE INTERNATIONAL MIGRATION POLICY PROGRAM

The movement of people has emerged as one of the critical issues facing the international community. Unless managed firmly but thoughtfully, migrations will pose critical challenges for democratic order and for international peace and stability. Against this backdrop, the International Migration Policy Program has developed a reputation as a leading source of expert analysis and policy ideas, as it focuses on bridging the worlds of immigration research and policy making and bringing an informed, independent voice to immigration policy debates here and abroad. The Program seeks to enhance the informed public's understanding of migration, refugee, and related topics and to shape the way policymakers think about and respond to these policy challenges. It does so by convening a series of breakfast briefings, luncheon seminars, policy roundtables, and study groups. Program staff also engage in an active schedule of writing and public speaking designed to promote a thoughtful and informed dialogue on this increasingly volatile policy area.

The Program also has convened an independent bilateral body, the U.S.-Mexico Consultative Group, to monitor and report on progress on cooperation in the areas of migration and labor within the NAFTA framework. Composed equally of U.S. and Mexican senior members of government, research, academic and advocacy organizations, the Consultative Group will candidly address the most intractable problems of border management and labor rights and standards.

The International Migration Policy Program receives funding for its activities from the Ford, MacArthur, Mellon, Sloan, and Tinker foundations.

Carnegie Endowment for International Peace
2400 N Street, N.W.,
Washington, D.C. 20037
Tel.: (202) 862-7900
Fax: (202) 862-2610
e-mail: ceip@igc.apc.org

Carnegie Moscow Center
Mosenka Plaza
24/27 Sadovaya-Samotechnaya
103051 Moscow, Russia
Tel: (7-095) 258-5025
Fax: (7-095) 258-5020
e-mail: carnegie@glas.apc.org

A NEW CARNEGIE ENDOWMENT SERIES ON
INTERNATIONAL MIGRATION ISSUES

To contribute constructively to the policy debate on immigration in the United States and abroad—and to help deepen policymaker and public understanding of the migration and refugee situation worldwide—the International Migration Policy Program of the Carnegie Endowment for International Peace announces a new series of policy papers.

Three policy papers, listed below, are now available. Future issues focus on how the United States should select skilled immigrants; migration policy issues in Australia, Canada, Germany, and Japan; progress toward freedom of movement within the European Union; and the sources of modern conceptions of democratic citizenship.

1. MANAGING UNCERTAINTY:
Regulating Immigration Flows in Advanced Industrial Countries

Demetrios G. Papademetriou and Kimberly Hamilton identify and analyze the conceptual problems and principal issues involved in thinking about and developing contemporary immigration policy regimes. They argue that policymakers must develop immigration policies that are at once effective in dealing with changing world conditions, capable of reaping immigration's benefits, able to sustain public support, and consistent with international commitments.

ISBN 0-87003-069-8   Price: $ 5.95

2. U.S. REFUGEE POLICY:
Dilemmas and Directions

Kathleen Newland reviews four major elements of the U.S. refugee program—resettlement, temporary protection, first asylum, and emergency response—and argues that, as practiced, these do not add up to a coherent refugee *policy*. Minimizing the need for refugee protection should be the central thrust of post-Cold War U.S. refugee policy. Nonetheless, the difficulty of preventing or resolving refugee-producing conflicts means that robust U.S. leadership in providing protection is still urgently needed.

ISBN 0-87003-071-x   Price: $ 5.95

3. CONVERGING PATHS TO RESTRICTION:
French, Italian, and British Responses to Immigration

In this study, Demetrios G. Papademetriou and Kimberly Hamilton, focus on how France, Italy, and the United Kingdom are responding to the complex issues raised by immigration and asylum matters. They explore the often trial-and-error character of governmental responses to these issues, the absence of mainstream political-party leadership, and the growing disjuncture between initiatives motivated by increasingly restrictionist impulses and practical efforts to further the immigrant integration at the local level.

ISBN 0-87003-073-6   Price: $6.95

For credit card orders, call Carnegie's distributor, The Brookings Institution, toll-free at 1-800-275-1447; in Washington, D.C., call 202-797-6258. Fax: 202-797-6004. When ordering, please refer to code RVCC.

9780870031168